Charlotte Mary Yonge

Aunt Charlotte's Roman History

Yonge, Charlotte Mary

Aunt Charlotte's Roman History

ISBN/EAN: 978-3-86741-509-5
First published in 2010 by Europaeischer Hochschulverlag GmbH & Co KG, Bremen, Germany.

© Europaeischer Hochschulverlag GmbH & Co KG, Fahrenheitstr. 1, D-28359 Bremen (www.ehv-online.com). All rights reserved.

This book is a reproduction of an out of print title and has originally been published in 1880. Because no electronic master copies of this title could be obtained, the publisher had to reuse old copies of the text. We therefore apologize for any possible loss in quality.

Charlotte Mary Yonge

Aunt Charlotte's Roman History

THE POPE'S DOORTENDER

PREFACE.

This sketch of the History of Rome covers the period till the reign of Charles the Great as head of the new Western Empire. The history has been given as briefly as could be done consistently with such details as can alone make it interesting to all classes of readers.

CHARLOTTE M. YONGE.

CONTENTS.

CHAPTER I. ITALY.	1
CHAPTER II. THE WANDERINGS OF ÆNEAS.	6
CHAPTER III. THE FOUNDING OF ROME. B.C. 753 — 713.	11
CHAPTER IV. NUMA AND TULLUS. B.C. 713 — 618.	16
CHAPTER V. THE DRIVING OUT OF THE TARQUINS. B.C. 578 — 309.	21
CHAPTER VI. THE WAR WITH PORSENA.	26
CHAPTER VII. THE ROMAN GOVERNMENT.	31
CHAPTER VIII. MENENIUS AGRIPPA'S FABLE. B.C. 494.	37
CHAPTER IX. CORIOLANUS AND CINCINNATUS. B.C. 458.	42
CHAPTER X. THE DECEMVIRS. B.C. 450.	47
CHAPTER XI. CAMILLUS' BANISHMENT. B.C. 390.	52
CHAPTER XII. THE SACK OF ROME. B.C. 390.	57
CHAPTER XIII. THE PLEBEIAN CONSULATE. B.C. 367.	62
CHAPTER XIV. THE DEVOTION OF DECIUS. B.C. 357	67
CHAPTER XV. THE SAMNITE WARS.	71
CHAPTER XVI. THE WAR WITH PYRRHUS. B.C. 280-271.	76
CHAPTER XVII. THE FIRST PUNIC WAR. 264-240.	81
CHAPTER XVIII. CONQUEST OF CISALPINE GAUL. 240-219.	87
CHAPTER XIX. THE SECOND PUNIC WAR. 219.	93
CHAPTER XX. THE FIRST EASTERN WAR. 215-183.	98
CHAPTER XXI. THE CONQUEST OF GREECE, CORINTH, AND CARTHAGE. 179 — 145.	102
CHAPTER XXII. THE GRACCHI. 137-122.	106
CHAPTER XXIII. THE WARS OF MARIUS. 106-98.	111
CHAPTER XXIV. THE ADVENTURES OF MARIUS. 93 — 84.	116
CHAPTER XXV. SULLA'S PROSCRIPTION. 88-71.	121

CHAPTER XXVI. THE CAREER OF POMPEIUS. 70-63.	126
CHAPTER XXVII. POMPEIUS AND CÆSAR. 61-48.	132
CHAPTER XXVIII. JULIUS CÆSAR. 48 – 44.	139
CHAPTER XXIX. THE SECOND TRIUMVIRATE. 44 – 33.	146
CHAPTER XXX. CÆSAR AUGUSTUS. B.C. 33 – A.D. 14.	153
CHAPTER XXXI. TIBERIUS AND CALIGULA. A.D. 14 – 41.	159
CHAPTER XXXII. CLAUDIUS AND NERO. A.D. 41-68.	165
CHAPTER XXXIII. THE FLAVIAN FAMILY. 62-96.	171
CHAPTER XXXIV. THE AGE OF THE ANTONINES. 96 – 194.	178
CHAPTER XXXV. THE PRÆTORIAN INFLUENCE. 197 – 284.	184
CHAPTER XXXVI. THE DIVISION OF THE EMPIRE. 284-312.	192
CHAPTER XXXVII. CONSTANTINE THE GREAT. 312-337.	198
CHAPTER XXXVIII. CONSTANTIUS. 337-364.	203
CHAPTER XXXIX. VALENTINIAN AND HIS FAMILY. 364-392.	208
CHAPTER XL. THEODOSIUS THE GREAT. 392-395.	214
CHAPTER XLI. ALARIC THE GOTH. 395-410.	219
CHAPTER XLII. THE VANDALS. 403.	224
CHAPTER XLIII. ATTILA THE HUN 435-457.	230
CHAPTER XLIV. THEODORIC THE OSTROGOTH. 457 – 561.	236
CHAPTER XLV. BELISARIUS. 533-563.	240
CHAPTER XLVI. POPE GREGORY THE GREAT. 563 – 800.	245

CHAPTER I.
ITALY.

I am going to tell you next about the most famous nation in the world. Going westward from Greece another peninsula stretches down into the Mediterranean. The Apennine Mountains run like a limb stretching out of the Alps to the south eastward, and on them seems formed that land, shaped somewhat like a leg, which is called Italy.

Round the streams that flowed down from these hills, valleys of fertile soil formed themselves, and a great many different tribes and people took up their abode there, before there was any history to explain their coming. Putting together what can be proved about them, it is plain, however, that most of them came of that old stock from which the Greeks descended, and to which we belong ourselves, and they spoke a language which had the same root as ours and as the Greek. From one of these nations the best known form of this, as it was polished in later times, was called Latin, from the tribe who spoke it.

THE TIBER

About the middle of the peninsula there runs down, westward from the Apennines, a river called the Tiber, flowing rapidly between seven low hills, which recede as it approaches the sea. One, in especial, called the Palatine Hill, rose separately, with a flat top and steep sides, about four hundred yards from the river, and girdled in by the other six. This was the place where the great Roman power grew up from beginnings, the truth of which cannot now be discovered.

CURIOUS POTTERY.

There were several nations living round these hills — the Etruscans, Sabines, and Latins being the chief. The homes of these nations seem to have been in the valleys round the spurs of the Apennines, where they had farms and fed their flocks; but above them was always the hill which they had fortified as strongly as possible, and where they took refuge if their enemies attacked them. The Etruscans built very mighty walls, and also managed the drainage of their cities wonderfully well. Many of their works remain to this day, and, in especial, their monuments have been opened, and the tomb of each chief has been found, adorned with figures of himself, half lying, half sitting; also curious pottery in red and black, from which something of their lives and ways is to be made out. They spoke a different language from what has become Latin, and they had a different religion, believing in one great Soul of the World, and also thinking much of rewards and punishments after death. But we know hardly anything about them, except that their chiefs were called Lucumos, and that they once had a wide power which they had lost before the time of history. The Romans called them Tusci, and Tuscany still keeps its name.

The Latins and the Sabines were more alike, and also more like the Greeks. There were a great many settlements of Greeks in the southern parts of Italy, and they learnt something from them. They had a great many gods. Every house had its own guardian. These were called Lares, or Penates, and were generally represented as little figures of dogs lying by the hearth, or as brass bars with dogs' heads. This is the reason that the bars which close in an open hearth are still called dogs. Whenever there was a meal in the house the master began by pouring out wine to the Lares, and also to his own ancestors, of whom he kept figures; for these natives thought much of their families, and all one family had the same name, like our surname, such as Tullius or Appius, the daughters only changing it by making it end in *a* instead of *us*, and the men having separate names standing first, such as Marcus or Lucius, though their sisters were only numbered to distinguish them.

Each city had a guardian spirit, each stream its nymph, each wood its faun; also there were gods to whom the boundary stones of estates were dedicated. There was a goddess of fruits called Pomona, and a god of fruits named Vertumnus. In their names the fields and the crops were solemnly blest, and all were sacred to Saturn. He, according to the old legends, had first taught husbandry, and when he reigned in Italy there was a golden age, when every one had his own field, lived by his own handiwork, and kept no slaves. There was a feast in honor of this time every year called the Saturnalia, when for a few days the slaves were all allowed to act as if they were free, and have all kinds of wild sports and merriment. Afterwards, when Greek learning came in,

Saturn was mixed up with the Greek Kronos, or Time, who devours his offspring, and the reaping-hook his figures used to carry for harvest became Time's scythe. The sky-god, Zeus or Deus Pater (or father), was shortened into Jupiter; Juno was his wife, and Mars was god of war, and in Greek times was supposed to be the same as Ares; Pallas Athene was joined with the Latin Minerva; Hestia, the goddess of the hearth, was called Vesta; and, in truth, we talk of the Greek gods by their Latin names. The old Greek tales were not known to the Latins in their first times, but only afterwards learnt from the Greeks. They seem to have thought of their gods as graver, higher beings, further off, and less capricious and fanciful than the legends about the weather had made them seem to the Greeks. Indeed, these Latins were a harder, tougher, graver, fiercer, more business-like race altogether than the Greeks; not so clever, thoughtful, or poetical, but with more of what we should now call sterling stuff in them.

At least so it was with that great nation which spoke their language, and seems to have been an offshoot from them. Rome, the name of which is said to mean the famous, is thought to have been at first a cluster of little villages, with forts to protect them on the hills, and temples in the forts. Jupiter had a temple on the Capitoline Hill, with cells for his worship, and that of Juno and Minerva; and the two-faced Janus, the god of gates, had his upon the Janicular Hill. Besides these, there were the Palatine, the Esquiline, the Aventine, the Cælian, and the Quirinal. The people of these villages called themselves Quirites, or spearmen, when they formed themselves into an army and made war on their neighbors, the Sabines and Latins, and by-and-by built a wall enclosing all the seven hills, and with a strip of ground within, free from houses, where sacrifices were offered and omens sought for.

JUPITER

The history of these people was not written till long after they had grown to be a mighty and terrible power, and had also picked up many Greek notions. Then they seem to have made their history backwards, and worked up their old stories and songs to explain the names and customs they found among them, and the tales they told were formed into a great history by one Titus Livius. It is needful to know these stories which every one used to believe to be really history; so we will tell them first, beginning, however, with a story told by the poet Virgil.

CHAPTER II.
THE WANDERINGS OF ÆNEAS.

You remember in the Greek history the burning of Troy, and how Priam and all his family were cut off. Among the Trojans there was a prince called Æneas, whose father was Anchises, a cousin of Priam, and his mother was said to be the goddess Venus. When he saw that the city was lost, he rushed back to his house, and took his old father Anchises on his back, giving him his Penates, or little images of household gods, to take care of, and led by the hand his little son Iulus, or Ascanius, while his wife Creusa followed close behind, and all the Trojans who could get their arms together joined him, so that they escaped in a body to Mount Ida; but just as they were outside the city he missed poor Creusa, and though he rushed back and searched for her everywhere, he never could find her. For the sake of his care for his gods, and for his old father, he is always known as the pious Æneas.

In the forests of Mount Ida he built ships enough to set forth with all his followers in quest of the new home which his mother, the goddess Venus, gave him hopes of. He had adventures rather like those of Ulysses as he sailed about the Mediterranean. Once in the Strophades, some clusters belonging to the Ionian Islands, when he and his troops had landed to get food, and were eating the flesh of the numerous goats which they found climbing about the rocks, down on them came the harpies, horrible birds with women's faces and hooked hands, with which they snatched away the food and spoiled what they could not eat. The Trojans shot at them, but the arrows glanced off their feathers and did not hurt them. However, they all flew off except one, who sat on a high rock, and croaked out that the Trojans would be punished for thus molesting the harpies by being tossed about till they should reach Italy, but there they should not build their city till they should have been so hungry as to eat their very trenchers.

They sailed away from this dismal prophetess, and touched on the coast of Epirus, where Æneas found his cousin Helenus, son to old Priam, reigning over a little new Troy, and married to

Andromache, Hector's wife, whom he had gained after Pyrrhus had been killed. Helenus was a prophet, and gave Æneas much advice. In especial he said that when the Trojans should come to Italy, they would find, under the holly-trees by the river side, a large white old sow lying on the ground, with a litter of thirty little pigs round her, and this should be a sign to them where they were to build their city.

By his advice the Trojans coasted round the south of Sicily, instead of trying to pass the strait between the dreadful Scylla and Charybdis, and just below Mount Etna an unfortunate man came running down to the beach begging to be taken in. He was a Greek, who had been left behind when Ulysses escaped from Polyphemus' cave, and had made his way to the forests, where he had lived ever since. They had just taken him in when they saw Cyclops coming down, with a pine tree for a staff, to wash the burning hollow of his lost eye in the sea, and they rowed off in great terror.

MOUNT ETNA.

Poor old Anchises died shortly after, and while his son was still sorrowing for him, Juno, who hated every Trojan, stirred up a terrible tempest, which drove the ships to the south, until, just as the sea began to calm down, they came into a beautiful bay, enclosed by tall cliffs with woods overhanging them. Here the tired wanderers landed, and, lighting a fire, Æneas went in quest of food. Coming out of the forest, they looked down from a hill, and beheld a multitude of people building a city, raising walls, houses, towers, and temples. Into one of these temples Æneas entered, and to his amazement he found the walls sculptured with all the story of the siege of Troy, and all his friends so perfectly represented, that he burst into tears at the sight.

Just then a beautiful queen, attended by a whole troop of nymphs, came into the temple. This lady was Dido; her husband, Sichæus, had been king of Tyre, till he was murdered by his brother Pygmalion, who meant to have married her, but she fled from him with a band of faithful Tyrians and all her husband's treasure, and had landed on the north coast of Africa. There she begged of the chief of the country as much land as could be enclosed by a bullock's hide. He granted this readily; and Dido, cutting the hide into the finest possible strips, managed to measure off with it ground enough to build the splendid city which she had named Carthage. She received Æneas most kindly, and took all his men into her city, hoping to keep them there for ever, and make him her husband. Æneas himself was so happy there, that he forgot all his plans and the prophecies he had heard, until Jupiter sent Mercury to rouse him to fulfil his destiny. He obeyed the call; and Dido was so wretched at his departure that she caused a great funeral pile to be built, laid herself on the top, and stabbed herself with Æneas' sword; the pile was burnt, and the Trojans saw the flame from their ships without knowing the cause.

CARTHAGE.

By-and-by Æneas landed at a place in Italy named Cumæ. There dwelt one of the Sybils. These were wondrous virgins whom Apollo had endowed with deep wisdom; and when Æneas went to consult the Cumæan Sybil, she told him that he must visit the under-world of Pluto to learn his fate. First, however, he had to go into a forest, and find there and gather a golden bough, which he was to bear in his hand to keep him safe. Long he sought it, until two doves, his mother's birds, came flying before him to show him the tree where gold gleamed through the boughs, and he found the branch growing on the tree as mistletoe grows on the thorn.

Guarded with this, and guided by the Sybil, after a great sacrifice, Æneas passed into a gloomy cave, where he came to the river Styx, round which flitted all the shades who had never received funeral rites, and whom the ferryman, Charon, would not carry over. The Sybil, however, made him take Æneas across, his boat groaning under the weight of a human body. On the other side stood Cerberus, but the Sybil threw him a cake of honey and of some opiate, and he lay asleep, while Æneas passed on and found in myrtle groves all who had died for love, among them, to his surprise, poor forsaken Dido. A little further on he found the home of the warriors, and held converse with his old Trojan friends. He passed by the place of doom for the wicked, Tartarus; and in the Elysian fields, full of laurel groves and meads of asphodel, he found the spirit of his father Anchises, and with him was allowed to see the souls of all their descendants, as yet unborn, who should raise the glory of their name. They are described on to the very time when the poet wrote to whom we owe all the tale of the wanderings of Æneas, namely, Virgil, who wrote the *Æneid*, whence all these stories are taken. He further tells us that Æneas landed in Italy just as his old nurse Caiëta died, at the place which is still called Gaëta. After they had buried her, they found a grove, where they sat down on the grass to eat, using large round cakes or biscuits to put their meat on. Presently they came to eating up the cakes. Little Ascanius cried out, "We are eating our very tables;" and Æneas, remembering the harpy's words, knew that his wanderings were over.

ROMAN SOLDIER.

CHAPTER III.
THE FOUNDING OF ROME.
B.C. 753 — 713.

Virgil goes on to tell at much length how the king of the country, Latinus, at first made friends with Æneas, and promised him his daughter Lavinia in marriage; but Turnus, an Italian chief who had before been a suitor to Lavinia, stirred up a great war, and was only captured and killed after much hard fighting. However, the white sow was found in the right place with all her little pigs, and on the spot was founded the city of Alba Longa, where Æneas and Lavinia reigned until he died, and his descendants, through his two sons, Ascanius or Iulus, and Æneas Silvius, reigned after him for fifteen generations.

The last of these fifteen was Amulius, who took the throne from his brother Numitor, who had a daughter named Rhea Silvia, a Vestal virgin. In Greece, the sacred fire of the goddess Vesta was tended by good men, but in Italy it was the charge of maidens, who were treated with great honor, but were never allowed to marry under pain of death. So there was great anger when Rhea Silvia became the mother of twin boys, and, moreover, said that her husband was the god Mars. But Mars did not save her from being buried alive, while the two babes were put in a trough on the waters of the river Tiber, there to perish. The river had overflowed its banks, and left the children on dry ground, where, however, they were found by a she-wolf, who fondled and fed them like her own offspring, until a shepherd met with them and took them home to his wife. She called them Romulus and Remus, and bred them up as shepherds.

When the twin brothers were growing into manhood, there was a fight between the shepherds of Numitor and Amulius, in which Romulus and Remus did such brave feats that they were led before Numitor. He enquired into their birth, and their foster-father told the story of his finding them, showing the trough in which they had been laid; and thus it became plain that they were the grandsons of Numitor. On finding this out, they collected an army, with which they drove away Amulius, and brought their grandfather back to Alba Longa.

They then resolved to build a new city for themselves on one of the seven low hills beneath which ran the yellow river Tiber; but they were not agreed on which hill to build, Remus wanting to build on the Aventine Hill, and Romulus on the Palatine. Their grandfather advised them to watch for omens from the gods, so each stood on his hill and watched for birds. Remus was the first to see six vultures flying, but Romulus saw twelve, and therefore the Palatine Hill was made the beginning of the city, and Romulus was chosen king. Remus was affronted, and when the mud wall was being raised around the space intended for the city, he leapt over it and laughed, whereupon Romulus struck him dead, crying out, "So perish all who leap over the walls of my city."

GLADIATORIAL SHOWS AT A BANQUET

Romulus traced out the form of the city with the plough, and made it almost a square. He called the name of it Rome, and lived in the midst of it in a mud-hovel, covered with thatch, in the midst of about fifty families of the old Trojan race, and a great many young men, outlaws and runaways from the neighboring states, who had joined him. The date of the building of Rome was supposed to be A.D. 753; and the Romans counted their years from it, as the Greeks did from the Olympiads, marking the date A.U.C., *anno urbis conditæ*, the year of the city being built. The youths who joined Romulus could not marry, as no one of the neighboring nations would give his daughter to one of these robbers, as they were esteemed. The nearest neighbors to Rome were the Sabines, and the Romans cast their eyes in vain on the Sabine ladies, till old Numitor advised Romulus to proclaim a great feast in honor of Neptune, with games and dances. All the people in the country round came to it, and when the revelry was at its height each of the unwedded Romans seized on a Sabine maiden and carried her away to his own house. Six hundred and eighty-three girls were thus seized, and the next day Romulus married them all after the fashion ever after observed in Rome. There was a great sacrifice, then each damsel was told, "Partake of your husband's fire and water;" he gave her a ring, and carried her over his threshold, where a sheepskin was spread, to show that her duty would be to spin wool for him, and she became his wife.

THE FORUM.

Romulus himself won his own wife, Hersilia, among the Sabines on this occasion; but the nation of course took up arms, under their king Tatius, to recover their daughters. Romulus drew out his troops into Campus Martius, or field of Mars, just beneath the Capitol, or great fort on the Saturnian Hill, and marched against the Sabines; but while he was absent, Tarpeia, the daughter of the governor of the little fort he had left on the Saturnian Hill, promised to let the Sabines in on condition they would give her what they wore on their left arms, meaning their bracelets; but they hated her treason even while they took advantage of it, and no sooner were they within the gate than they pelted her with their heavy shields, which they wore on their left arms, and killed her. The cliff on the top of which she died is still called the Tarpeian rock, and criminals were executed by being thrown from the top of it. Romulus tried to regain the Capitol, but the Sabines rolled down stones on the Romans, and he was stunned by one that struck him on the head; and though he quickly recovered and rallied his men, the battle was going against him, when all the Sabine women, who had been nearly two years Roman wives, came rushing out, with their little children in their arms and their hair flying, begging their fathers and husbands not to kill one another. This led to the making of a peace, and it was agreed that the Sabines and Romans should make but one nation, and that Romulus and Tatius should reign together at Rome. Romulus lived on the Palatine Hill, Tatius on the Tarpeian, and the valley between was called the Forum, and was the market-place, and also the spot where all public assemblies were held. All the chief arrangements for war and government were believed by the Romans to have been laws of Romulus. However, after five years, Tatius was murdered at a place called Lavinium, in the middle of a sacrifice, and Romulus reigned alone till in the middle of a great assembly of his soldiers outside the city, a storm of thunder and lightning came on, and every one hurried home, but the king was nowhere to be found; for, as some say, his father Mars had come down in the tempest and carried him away to reign with the gods, while others declared that he was murdered by persons, each of whom carried home a fragment of his body that it might never be found. It matters less which way we tell it, since the story of Romulus was quite as much a fable as that of Æneas; only it must be remembered as the Romans themselves believed it. They worshipped Romulus under the name of Quirinus, and called their chief families Quirites, both words coming from *ger* (a spear); and the she-wolf and twins were the favorite badge of the empire. The Capitoline Hill, the Palatine, and the Forum all still bear the same names.

CHAPTER IV.
NUMA AND TULLUS.
B.C. 713 — 618.

It was understood between the Romans and the Sabines that they should have by turns a king from each nation, and, on the disappearance of Romulus, a Sabine was chosen, named Numa Pompilius, who had been married to Tatia, the daughter of the Sabine king Tatius, but she was dead, and had left one daughter. Numa had, ever since her death, been going about from one grove or fountain sacred to the gods to another offering up sacrifices, and he was much beloved for his gentleness and wisdom. There was a grove near Rome, in a valley, where a fountain gushed forth from the rock; and here Egeria, the nymph of the stream, in the shade of the trees, counselled Numa on his government, which was so wise that he lived at peace with all his neighbors. When the Romans doubted whether it was really a goddess who inspired him, Egeria convinced them, for the next time he had any guests in his house, the earthenware plates with homely fare on them were changed before their eyes into golden dishes with dainty food. Moreover, there was brought from heaven a bronze shield, which was to be carefully kept, since Rome would never fall while it was safe. Numa had eleven other shields like it made and hung in the temple of Mars, and, yearly, a set of men dedicated to the office bore them through the city with songs and dances. Just as all warlike customs were said to have been invented by Romulus, all peaceful and religious ones were held to have sprung from Numa and his Egeria. He was said to have fixed the calendar and invented the names of the months, and to have built an altar to Good Faith to teach the Romans to keep their word to one another and to all nations, and to have dedicated the bounds of each estate to the Dii Termini, or Landmark Gods, in whose honor there was a feast yearly. He also was said to have had such power with Jupiter as to have persuaded him to be content without receiving sacrifices of men and women. In short, all the better things in the Roman system were supposed to be due to the gentle Numa.

At the gate called Janiculum stood a temple to the watchman god Janus, whose figure had two faces, and held the keys, and after whom was named the month January. His temple was always open in time of war, and closed in time of peace. Numa's reign was counted as the first out of only three times in Roman history that it was shut.

JANUS.

Numa was said to have reigned thirty-eight years, and then he gradually faded away, and was buried in a stone coffin outside the Janicular gate, all the books he had written being, by his desire, buried with him. Egeria wept till she became a fountain in her own valley; and so ended what in Roman faith answered to the golden age of Greece.

The next king was of Roman birth, and was named Tullus Hostilius. He was a great warrior, and had a war with the Albans until it was agreed that the two cities should join together in one, as the Romans and Sabines had done before; but there was a dispute which should be the greater city in the league and it was determined to settle it by a combat. In each city there was a family where three sons had been born at a birth, and their mothers were sisters. Both sets were of the same age — fine young men, skilled in weapons; and it was agreed that the six should fight together, the three whose family name was Horatius on the Roman side, the three called Curiatius on the Alban side, and whichever set gained the mastery was to give it to his city.

They fought in the plain between the camps, and very hard was the strife until two of the Horatii were killed and all the three Curiatii were wounded, but the last Horatius was entirely untouched. He began to run, and his cousins pursued him, but at different distances, as one was less hindered by his wound than the others. As soon as the first came up. Horatius slew him, and so the second and the third: as he cut down this last he cried out, "To the glory of Rome I sacrifice thee." As the Alban king saw his champion fall, he turned to Tullus Hostilius and asked what his commands were. "Only to have the Alban youth ready when I need them," said Tullus.

A wreath was set on the victor's head, and, loaded with the spoil of the Curiatii, he was led into the city in triumph. His sister came hurrying to meet him; she was betrothed to one of the Curiatii, and was in agony to know his fate; and when she saw the garment she had spun for him hanging blood-stained over her brother's shoulders, she burst into loud lamentations. Horatius, still hot with fury, struck her dead on the spot, crying, "So perish every Roman who mourns the death of an enemy of his country." Even her father approved the cruel deed, and would not bury her in his family tomb — so stern were Roman feelings, putting the honor of the country above everything. However, Horatius was brought before the king for the murder, and was sentenced to die; but the people entreated that their champion might be spared, and he was only made to pass under what was called the yoke, namely, spears set up like a doorway.

Tullus Hostilius gained several victories over his neighbors, but he was harsh and presuming, and offended the gods, and, when he was using some spell such as good Numa had used to hold converse with Jupiter, the angry god sent lightning and burnt up him and his family. The people then chose Ancus Martins, the son of Numa's daughter, who is said to have ruled in his grandfather's spirit, though he could not avoid wars with the Latins. The first bridge over the Tiber, named the Sublician, was said to have been built by him. In his time there came to Rome a family called Tarquin. Their father was a Corinthian, who had settled in an Etruscan town named Tarquinii, whence came the family name. He was said to have first taught writing in Italy, and, indeed, the Roman letters which we still use are Greek letters made simpler. His eldest son, finding that because of his foreign blood he could rise to no honors in Etruria, set off with his wife Tanaquil, and their little son Lucius Tarquinius, to settle in Rome. Just as they came in sight of Rome, an eagle swooped down from the sky, snatched off little Tarquin's cap, and flew up with it, but the next moment came down again and put it back on his head. On this Tanaquil foretold that her son would be a great king, and he became so famous a warrior when he grew up, that, as the children of Ancus were too young to reign at their father's death, he was chosen king. He is said to have been the first Roman king who wore a purple robe and golden crown, and in the valley between the Palatine and Aventine Hills he made a circus, where games could be held like those of the Greeks; also he placed stone benches and stalls for shops round the Forum, and built a stone wall instead of a mud one round the city. He is commonly called Tarquinus Priscus, or the elder.

There was a fair slave girl in his house, who was offering cakes to Lar, the household spirit, when he appeared to her in bodily form. When she told the king's mother, Tanaquil, she said it was a token that he wanted to marry her, and arrayed her as a bride for him. Of this marriage there sprang a boy called Servius Tullus. When this child lay asleep, bright flames played about his head, and Tanaquil knew he would be great, so she caused her son Tarquin to give him his daughter in marriage when he grew up.

ACTORS

This greatly offended the two sons of Ancus Martius, and they hired two young men to come before him as wood-cutters, with axes over their shoulders, pretending to have a quarrel about some goats, and while he was listening to their cause they cut him down and mortally wounded him. He had lost his sons, and had only two baby grandsons, Aruns and Tarquin, who could not reign as yet; but while he was dying, Tanaquil stood at the window and declared that he was only stunned and would soon be well. This, as she intended, so frightened the sons of Ancus that they fled from Rome; and Servius Tullus, coming forth in the royal robes, was at once hailed as king by all the people of Rome, being thus made king that he might protect his wife's two young nephews, the two little Tarquins.

CHAPTER V.
THE DRIVING OUT OF THE TARQUINS.
B.C. 578 — 309.

Servius Tullus was looked on by the Romans as having begun making their laws, as Romulus had put their warlike affairs in order, and Numa had settled their religion. The Romans were all in great clans or families, all with one name, and these were classed in tribes. The nobler ones, who could count up from old Trojan, Latin, or Sabine families, were called Patricians — from *pater*, a father — because they were fathers of the people; and the other families were called Plebeian, from *plebs*, the people. The patricians formed the Senate or Council of Government, and rode on horseback in war, while the plebeians fought on foot. They had spears, round shields, and short pointed swords, which cut on each side of the blade. Tullus is said to have fixed how many men of each tribe should be called out to war. He also walled in the city again with a wall five miles round; and he made many fixed laws, one being that when a man was in debt his goods might be seized, but he himself might not be made a slave. He was the great friend of the plebeians, and first established the rule that a new law of the Senate could not be made without the consent of the Comitia, or whole free people.

The Sabines and Romans were still striving for the mastery, and a husbandman among the Sabines had a wonderfully beautiful cow. An oracle declared that the man who sacrificed this cow to Diana upon the Aventine Hill would secure the chief power to his nation. The Sabine drove the cow to Rome, and was going to kill her, when a crafty Roman priest told him that he must first wash his hands in the Tiber, and while he was gone sacrificed the cow himself, and by this trick secured the rule to Rome. The great horns of the cow were long after shown in the temple of Diana on the Aventine, where Romans, Sabines, and Latins every year joined in a great sacrifice.

The two daughters of Servius were married to their cousins, the two young Tarquins. In each pair there was a fierce and a gentle one. The fierce Tullia was the wife of the gentle Aruns

Tarquin; the gentle Tulla had married the proud Lucius Tarquin. Aruns' wife tried to persuade her husband to seize the throne that had belonged to his father, and when he would not listen to her, she agreed with his brother Lucius that, while he murdered her sister, she should kill his brother, and then that they should marry. The horrid deed was carried out, and old Servius, seeing what a wicked pair were likely to come after him, began to consider with the Senate whether it would not be better to have two consuls or magistrates chosen every year than a king. This made Lucius Tarquin the more furious, and going to the Senate, where the patricians hated the king as the friend of the plebeians, he stood upon the throne, and was beginning to tell the patricians that this would be the ruin of their greatness, when Servius came in and, standing on the steps of the doorway, ordered him to come down. Tarquin sprang on the old man and hurled him backward, so that the fall killed him, and his body was left in the street. The wicked Tullia, wanting to know how her husband had sped, came out in her chariot on that road. The horses gave back before the corpse. She asked what was in their way; the slave who drove her told her it was the king's body. "Drive on," she said. The horrid deed caused the street to be known ever after as "Sceleratus," or the wicked. But it was the plebeians who mourned for Servius; the patricians in their anger made Tarquin king, but found him a very hard and cruel master, so that he is generally called Tarquinius Superbus, or Tarquin the proud. In his time the Sybil of Cumæ, the same wondrous maiden of deep wisdom who had guided Æneas to the realms of Pluto, came, bringing nine books of prophecies of the history of Rome, and offered them to him at a price which he thought too high, and refused. She went away, destroyed three, and brought back the other six, asking for them double the price of the whole. He refused. She burnt three more, and brought him the last three with the price again doubled, because the fewer they were, the more precious. He bought them at last, and placed them in the Capitol, whence they were now and then taken to be consulted as oracles.

SYBIL'S CAVE.

Rome was at war with the city of Gabii, and as the city was not to be subdued by force, Tarquin tried treachery. His eldest son, Sextus Tarquinius, fled to Gabii, complaining of ill-usage of his father, and showing marks of a severe scourging. The Gabians believed him, and he was soon so much trusted by them as to have the whole command of the army and manage everything in the city. Then he sent a messenger to his father to ask what he was to do next. Tarquin was walking through a cornfield. He made no answer in words, but with a switch cut off the heads of all the poppies and taller stalks of corn, and bade the messenger tell Sextus what he had seen. Sextus understood, and contrived to get all the chief men of Gabii exiled or put to death, and without them the city fell an easy prey to the Romans.

Tarquin sent his two younger sons and their cousin to consult the oracle at Delphi, and with them went Lucius Junius, who was called Brutus because he was supposed to be foolish, that being the meaning of the word; but his folly was only put on, because he feared the jealousy of his cousins. After doing their father's errand, the two Tarquins asked who should rule Rome after their father. "He," said the priestess, "who shall first kiss his mother on his return." The two brothers agreed that they would keep this a secret from their elder brother Sextus, and, as soon as they reached home, both of them rushed into the women's rooms, racing each to be the first to embrace their mother Tullia; but at the very entrance of Rome Brutus pretended to slip, threw himself on the ground and kissed his Mother Earth, having thus guessed the right meaning of the answer.

He waited patiently, however, and still was thought a fool when the army went out to besiege the city of Ardea; and while the troops were encamped round it, some of the young patricians began to dispute which had the best wife. They agreed to put it to the test by galloping late in the evening to look in at their homes and see what their wives were about. Some were idling, some were visiting, some were scolding, some were dressing, some were asleep; but at Collatia, the farm of another of the Tarquin family, thence called Collatinus, they found his beautiful wife Lucretia among her maidens spinning the wool of the flocks. All agreed that she was the best of wives; but the wicked Sextus Tarquin only wanted to steal her from her husband, and going by night to Collatia, tried to make her desert her lord, and when she would not listen to him he ill-treated her cruelly, and told her that he should accuse her to her husband. She was so overwhelmed with grief and shame that in the morning she sent for her father and husband, told them all that that happened, and saying that she could not bear life after being so put to shame, she drew out a dagger and stabbed herself before their eyes — thinking, as all these heathen Romans did, that it was better to die by one's own hand than to live in disgrace.

Lucius Brutus had gone to Collatia with his cousin, and while Collatinus and his father-in-law stood horror-struck, he called to them to revenge this crime. Snatching the dagger from Lucretia's breast, he galloped to Rome, called the people together in the Forum, and, holding up the bloody weapon in his hand, he made them a speech, asking whether they would any longer endure such a family of tyrants. They all rose as one man, and choosing Brutus himself and Collatinus to be their leaders, as the consuls whom Servius Tullus had thought of making, they shut the gates of Rome, and would not open them when Tarquin and his sons would have returned. So ended the kingdom of Rome.

CHAPTER VI.
THE WAR WITH PORSENA.

From the time of the flight of the Tarquins, Rome was governed by two consuls, who wore all the tokens of royalty except the crown. Tarquin fled into Etruria, whence his grandfather had come, and thence tried to obtain admission into Rome. The two young sons of Brutus and the nephews of Collatinus were drawn into a plot for bringing them back again, and on its discovery were brought before the two consuls. Their guilt was proved, and their father sternly asked what they had to say in their defence. They only wept, and so did Collatinus and many of the senators, crying out, "Banish them, banish them." Brutus, however, as if unmoved, bade the executioners do their office. The whole Senate shrieked to hear a father thus condemn his own children, but he was resolute, and actually looked on while the young men were first scourged and then beheaded.

Collatinus put off the further judgment in hopes to save his nephews, and Brutus told them that he had put them to death by his own power as a father, but that he left the rest to the voice of the people, and they were sent into banishment. Even Collatinus was thought to have acted weakly, and was sent into exile — so determined were the Romans to have no one among them who would not uphold their decrees to the utmost. Tarquin advanced to the walls and cut down all the growing corn around the Campus Martius and threw it into the Tiber; there it formed a heap round which an island was afterwards formed. Brutus himself and his cousin Aruns Tarquin soon after killed one another in single combat in a battle outside the walls, and all the women of Rome mourned for him as for a father.

Tarquin found a friend in the Etruscan king called Lars Porsena, who brought an army to besiege Rome and restore him to the throne. He advanced towards the gate called Janiculum upon the Tiber, and drove the Romans out of the fort on the other side the river. The Romans then retreated across the bridge, placing three men to guard it until all should be gone over and it could be broken down.

BRUTUS CONDEMNING HIS SONS.

There stood the brave three — Horatius, Lartius, and Herminius — guarding the bridge while their fellow-citizens were fleeing across it, three men against a whole army. At last the weapons of Lartius and Herminius were broken down, and Horatius bade them hasten over the bridge while it could still bear their weight. He himself fought on till he was wounded in the thigh, and the last timbers of the bridge were falling into the stream. Then spreading out his arms, he called upon Father Tiber to receive him, leapt into the river and swam across amid a shower of arrows, one of which put out his eye, and he was lame for life. A statue of him "halting on his thigh" was set up in the temple of Vulcan, and he was rewarded with as much land as one yoke of oxen could plough in a day, and the 300,000 citizens of Rome each gave him a day's provision of corn.

Porsena then blockaded the city, and when the Romans were nearly starving he sent them word that he would give them food if they would receive their old masters; but they made answer that hunger was better than slavery, and still held out. In the midst of their distress, a young man named Caius Mucius came and begged leave of the consuls to cross the Tiber and go to attempt something to deliver his country. They gave leave, and creeping through the Etruscan camp he came into the king's tent just as Porsena was watching his troops pass by in full order. One of his counsellors was sitting beside him so richly dressed that Mucius did not know which was king, and leaping towards them, he stabbed the counsellor to the heart. He was seized at once and dragged before the king, who fiercely asked who he was, and what he meant by such a crime.

The young man answered that his name was Caius Mucius, and that he was ready to do and dare anything for Rome. In answer to threats of torture, he quietly stretched out his right hand and thrust it into the flame that burnt in a brazier close by, holding it there without a sign of pain, while he bade Porsena see what a Roman thought of suffering.

Porsena was so struck that he at once gave the daring man his life, his freedom, and even his dagger; and Mucius then told him that three hundred youths like himself had sworn to have his life unless he left Rome to her liberty. This was false, but both the lie and the murder were for Rome's sake; they were both admired by the Romans, who held that the welfare of their city was their very first duty. Mucius could never use his right hand again, and was always called Scævola, or the Left-handed, a name that went on to his family.

Porsena believed the story, and began to make peace. A truce was agreed on, and ten Roman youths and as many girls were given up to the Etruscans as hostages. While the conferences were going on, one of the Roman girls named Clelia forgot her duty so much as to swim home across the river with all her companions; but Valeria, the consul's daughter, was received with all the anger that breach of trust deserved, and her father mounted his horse at once to take the party back again. Just as they reached the Etruscan camp, the Tarquin father and brothers, and a whole troop of the enemy, fell on them. While the consul was fighting against a terrible force, Valeria dashed on into the camp and called out Porsena and his son. They, much grieved that the truce should have been broken, drove back their own men, and were so angry with the Tarquins as to give up their cause. He asked which of the girls had contrived the escape, and when Clelia confessed it was herself, he made her a present of a fine horse and its trappings, which she little deserved.

This Valerius was called Publicola, or the people's friend. He died a year or two later, after so many victories that the Romans honored him among their greatest heroes. Tarquin still continued to seek support among the different Italian nations, and again attacked the Romans with the help of the Latins. The chief battle was fought close to Lake Regillus; Aulus Posthumius was the commander, but Marcus Valerius, brother to Publicola, was general of the horse. He had vowed to build a temple to Castor and Pollux if the Romans gained the victory; and in the beginning of the fight, two glorious youths of god-like stature appeared on horseback at the head of the Roman horse and fought for them. It was a very hard-fought battle. Valerius was killed, but so was Titus Tarquin, and the Latin force was entirely broken and routed. That same evening the two youths rode into the Forum, their horses dripping with sweat and their weapons bloody. They drew up and washed themselves at a fountain near the temple of Vesta, and as the people crowded round they told of the great victory, and while one man named Domitius doubted of it, since the Lake Regillus was too far off for tidings to have come so fast, one of them laid his hand on the doubter's beard and changed it in a moment from black to copper color, so that he came to be called Domitius Ahenobarbus, or Brazen-beard. Then they disappeared, and the next morning Posthumius' messenger brought the news. The Romans had no doubt that these were indeed the glorious twins, and built their temple, as Valerius had vowed.

ROMAN ENSIGNS, STANDARDS, TRUMPETS ETC.

Tarquin had lost all his sons, and died in wretched exile at Cumæ. And here ends what is looked on as the legendary history of Rome, for though most of these stories have dates, and some sound possible, there is so much that is plainly untrue mixed up with them, that they can only be looked on as the old stories which were handed down to account for the Roman customs and copied by their historians.

CHAPTER VII.
THE ROMAN GOVERNMENT.

So far as true history can guess, the Romans really did have kings and drove them out, but there are signs that, though Porsena was a real king, the war was not so honorable to the Romans as they said, for he took the city and made them give up all their weapons to him, leaving them nothing but their tools for husbandry. But they liked to forget their misfortunes.

The older Roman families were called patricians, or fathers, and thought all rights to govern belonged to them. Settlers who came in later were called plebeians, or the people, and at first had no rights at all, for all the land belonged to the patricians, and the only way for the plebeians to get anything done for them was to become hangers-on — or, as they called it, clients — of some patrician who took care of their interests. There was a council of patricians called the Senate, chosen among themselves, and also containing by right all who had been chief magistrates. The whole assembly of the patricians was called the Comitia. They, as has been said before, fought on horseback, while the plebeians fought on foot; but out of the rich plebeians a body was formed called the knights, who also used horses, and wore gold rings like the patricians.

But the plebeians were always trying not to be left out of everything. By and by, they said under Servius Tullius, the city was divided into six quarters, and all the families living in them into six tribes, each of which had a tribune to watch over it, bring up the number of its men, and lead them to battle. Another division of the citizens, both patrician and plebeian, was made every five years. They were all counted and numbered and divided off into centuries according to their wealth. Then these centuries, or hundreds, had votes, by the persons they chose, when it was a question of peace or war.

HEAD OF JUPITER.

Their meeting was called the Comitia; but as there were more patrician centuries than plebeian ones, the patricians still had much more power. Besides, the Senate and all the magistrates were in those days always patricians. These magistrates were chosen every year. There were two consuls, who were like kings for the time, only that they wore no crowns; they had purple robes, and sat in chairs ornamented with ivory, and they were always attended by lictors, who carried bundles of rods tied round an axe — the first for scourging, the second for beheading. There were under them two prætors, or judges, who tried offences; two quæstors, who attended to the public buildings; and two censors, who had to look after the numbering and registering of the people in their tribes and centuries. The consuls in general commanded the army, but sometimes, when there was a great need, one single leader was chosen and was called dictator.

Sometimes a dictator was chosen merely to fulfil an omen, by driving a nail into the head of the great statue of Jupiter in the Capitol. Besides these, all the priests had to be patricians; the chief of all was called Pontifex Maximus. Some say this was because he was the *fax* (maker) of *pontes* (bridges), as he blessed them and decided by omens where they should be; but others think the word was Pompifex, and that he was the maker of pomps or ceremonies. There were many priests as well as augurs, who had to draw omens from the flight of birds or the appearance of sacrifices, and who kept the account of the calendar of lucky and unlucky days, and of festivals.

FEMALE COSTUMES.

The Romans were a grave religious people in those days, and did not count their lives or their affections dear in comparison with their duties to their altars and their hearths, though their notions of duty do not always agree with ours. Their dress in the city was a white woollen garment edged with purple — it must have been more like in shape to a Scottish plaid than anything else — and was wrapped round so as to leave one arm free: sometimes a fold was drawn over the head. No one might wear it but a free-born Roman, and he never went out on public business without it, even when more convenient fashions had been copied from Greece. Those who were asking votes for a public office wore it white (*candidus*), and therefore were called candidates. The consuls had it on great days entirely purple and embroidered, and all senators and ex-magistrates had broader borders of purple. The ladies wore a long graceful wrapping-gown; the boys a short tunic, and round their necks was hung a hollow golden ball called a *bulla*, or bubble. When a boy was seventeen, there was a great family sacrifice to the Lares and the forefathers, his bulla was taken off, the toga was put on, and he was enrolled by his own prænomen, Caius or Lucius, or whatever it might be, for there was only a choice of fifteen. After this he was liable to be called out to fight. A certain number of men were chosen from each tribe by the tribune. It was divided into centuries, each led by a centurion; and the whole body together was called a legion, from *lego*, to choose. In later times the proper number for a legion was 6000 men. Each legion had a standard, a bar across the top of the spear, with the letters on it S P Q R — *Senatus, Populus Que Romanus* — meaning the Roman Senate and People, a purple flag below and a figure above, such as an eagle, or the wolf and twins, or some emblem dear to the Romans. The legions were on foot, but the troops of patricians and knights on horseback were attached to them and had to protect them.

The Romans had in those days very small riches, they held in general small farms in the country, which they worked themselves with the help of their sons and slaves. The plebeians were often the richest. They too held farms leased to them by the state, and had often small shops in Rome. The whole territory was so small that it was easy to come into Rome to worship, attend the

Senate, or vote, and many had no houses in the city. Each man was married with a ring and sacrifice, and the lady was then carried over the threshold, on which a sheepskin was spread, and made mistress of the house by being bidden to be Caia to Caius.

FEMALE COSTUMES.

The Roman matrons were good and noble women in those days, and the highest praise of them was held to be *Domum mansit, lanam fecit* — she stayed at home and spun wool. Each man was absolute master in his own house, and had full power over his grown-up sons, even for life or death, and they almost always submitted entirely. For what made the Romans so great was that they were not only brave, but they were perfectly obedient, and obeyed as perfectly as they could their fathers, their officers, their magistrates, and, as they thought, their gods.

CHAPTER VIII.
MENENIUS AGRIPPA'S FABLE.
B.C. 494.

A great deal of the history of Rome consists of struggles between the patricians and plebeians. In those early days the plebeians were often poor, and when they wanted to improve their lands they had to borrow money from the patricians, who not only had larger lands, but, as they were the officers in war, got a larger share of the spoil. The Roman law was hard on a man in debt. His lands might be seized, he might be thrown into prison or sold into slavery with his wife and children, or, if the creditors liked, be cut to pieces so that each might take his share.

One of these debtors, a man who was famous for bravery as a centurion, broke out of his prison and ran into the Forum, all in rags and with chains still hanging to his hands and feet, showing them to his fellow-citizens, and asking if this was just usage of a man who had done no crime. They were very angry, and the more because one of the consuls, Appius Claudius, was known to be very harsh, proud and cruel, as indeed were all his family. The Volscians, a tribe often at war with them, broke into their land at the same time, and the Romans were called to arms, but the plebeians refused to march until their wrongs were redressed. On this the other consul, Servilius, promised that a law should be made against keeping citizens in prison for debt or making slaves of their children; and thereupon the army assembled, marched against the enemy, and defeated them, giving up all the spoil to his troops. But the senate, when the danger was over, would not keep its promises, and even appointed a Dictator to put the plebeians down. Thereupon they assembled outside the walls in a strong force, and were going to attack the patricians, when the wise old Menenius Agrippa was sent out to try to pacify them. He told them a fable, namely, that once upon a time all the limbs of a man's body became disgusted with the service they had to render to the belly. The feet and legs carried it about, the hands worked for it and carried food to it, the mouth ate for it, and so on. They thought it hard thus all to toil for it, and agreed to do nothing for it — neither to carry it about, clothe it, nor feed it. But soon all found themselves growing weak and starved, and were obliged to own that all would perish together unless they went on waiting on this seemingly useless belly. So Agrippa told them that all ranks and states depended on one another, and unless all worked together all must be confusion and go to decay. The fable seems to have convinced both rich and poor; the debtors were set free and the debts forgiven. And though the laws about debts do not seem to have been changed, another law was made which gave the plebeians tribunes in peace as well as war. These tribunes were always to be plebeians, chosen by their own fellows. No one was allowed to hurt them during their year of office, on pain of being declared accursed and losing his property; and they had the power of stopping any decision of the senate by saying solemnly, *Veto*, I forbid. They were called tribunes of the people, while the officers in war were called military tribunes; and as it was on the Mons Sacer, or Sacred Mount, that this was settled, these laws were called the *Leges Sacrariæ*. An altar to the Thundering Jupiter was built to consecrate them: and, in gratitude for his management, Menenius Agrippa was highly honored all his life, and at his death had a public funeral.

But the struggles of the plebeians against the patricians were not by any means over. The Roman land — Agri (acre), it was called — had at first been divided in equal shares — at least so it was said — but as belonging to the state all the time, and only held by the occupier. As time went on, some persons of course gathered more into their own hands, and others of spendthrift or unfortunate families became destitute. Then there was an outcry that, as the lands belonged to the whole state, it ought to take them all back and divide them again more equally: but the patricians naturally regarded themselves as the owners, and would not hear of this scheme, which we shall hear of again and again by the name of the Agrarian Law. One of the patricians, who had thrice been consul, by name Spurius Cassius, did all he could to bring it about, but though the law was passed he could not succeed in getting it carried out. The patricians hated him, and a report got abroad that he was only gaining favor with the people in order to get himself made king. This made even the plebeians turn against him as a traitor; he was condemned by the whole assembly of the people, and beheaded, after being scourged by the lictors. The people soon mourned for their friend, and felt that they had been deceived in giving him up to their enemies. The senate would not execute his law, and the plebeians would not enlist in the next war, though the senate threatened to cut down the fruit trees and destroy the crops of every man who refused to join the army. When they were absolutely driven into the ranks, they even refused to draw their swords in face of the enemy, and would not gain a victory lest their consul should have the honor of it.

SENATORIAL PALACE.

This consul's name was Kæso Fabius. He belonged to a very clever, wary family, whose name it was said was originally *Foveus* (ditch), because they had first devised a plan of snaring wolves in pits or ditches. They were thought such excellent defenders of the claims of the patricians that for seven years following one or other of the Fabii was chosen consul. But by-and-by they began either to see that the plebeians had rights, or that they should do best by siding with them, for they went over to them; and when Kæso next was consul he did all he could to get the laws of Cassius carried out, but the senate were furious with him, and he found it was not safe to stay in Rome when his consulate was over. So he resolved at any rate to do good to his country. The Etruscans often came over the border and ravaged the country; but there was a watch-tower on the banks of the little river Cremera, which flows into the Tiber, and Fabius offered, with all the men of his name — 306 in number, and 4000 clients — to keep guard there against the enemy. For some time they prospered there, and gained much spoil from the Etruscans; but at last the whole Etruscan army came against them, showing only a small number at first to tempt them out to fight, then falling on them with the whole force and killing the whole of them, so that of the whole name there remained only one boy of fourteen who had been left behind at Rome. And what was worse, the consul, Titus Menenius, was so near the army that he could have saved the Fabii, but for the hatred the patricians bore them as deserters from their cause.

VIEW OF A ROMAN HARBOR.

However, the tribune Publilius gained for the plebeians that there should be five tribunes instead of two, and made a change in the manner of electing them which prevented the patricians from interfering. Also it was decreed that to interrupt a tribune in a public speech deserved death. But whenever an Appius Claudius was consul he took his revenge, and was cruelly severe, especially in the camp, where the consul as general had much more power than in Rome. Again the angry plebeians would not fight, but threw down their arms in sight of the enemy. Claudius scourged and beheaded; they endured grimly and silently, knowing that when he returned to Rome and his consulate was over their tribunes would call him to account. And so they did, and before all the tribes of Rome summoned him to answer for his savage treatment of free Roman citizens. He made a violent answer, but he saw how it would go with him, and put himself to death to avoid the sentence. So were the Romans proving again and again the truth of Agrippa's parable, that nothing can go well with body or members unless each will be ready to serve the other.

CHAPTER IX.
CORIOLANUS AND CINCINNATUS.
B.C. 458.

All the time these struggles were going on between the patricians and the plebeians at home, there were wars with the neighboring tribes, the Volscians, the Veians, the Latins, and the Etruscans. Every spring the fighting men went out, attacked their neighbors, drove off their cattle, and tried to take some town; then fought a battle, and went home to reap the harvest, gather the grapes and olives in the autumn, and attend to public business and vote for the magistrates in the winter. They were small wars, but famous men fought in them. In a war against the Volscians, when Cominius was consul, he was besieging a city called Corioli, when news came that the men of Antium were marching against him, and in their first attack on the walls the Romans were beaten off, but a gallant young patrician, descended from the king Ancus Marcius, Caius Marcius by name, rallied them and led them back with such spirit that the place was taken before the hostile army came up; then he fought among the foremost and gained the victory. When he was brought to the consul's tent covered with wounds, Cominius did all he could to show his gratitude — set on the young man's head the crown of victory, gave him the surname of Coriolanus in honor of his exploits, and granted him the tenth part of the spoil of ten prisoners. Of them, however, Coriolanus only accepted one, an old friend of the family, whom he set at liberty at once. Afterwards, when there was a great famine in Rome, Coriolanus led an expedition to Antium, and brought away quantities of corn and cattle, which he distributed freely, keeping none for himself.

But though he was so free of hand, Coriolanus was a proud, shy man, who would not make friends with the plebeians, and whom the tribunes hated as much as he despised them. He was elected consul, and the tribunes refused to permit him to become one; and when a shipload of wheat arrived from Sicily, there was a fierce quarrel as to how it should be distributed. The tribunes impeached him before the people for withholding it from them, and by the vote of a large number of citizens he was banished from Roman lands. His anger was great, but quiet. He went without a word away from the Forum to his house, where he took leave of his mother Veturia, his wife Volumnia, and his little children, and then went and placed himself by the hearth of Tullus the Volscian chief, in whose army he meant to fight to revenge himself upon his countrymen.

Together they advanced upon the Roman territory, and after ravaging the country threatened to besiege Rome. Men of rank came out and entreated him to give up this wicked and cruel vengeance, and to have pity on his friends and native city; but he answered that the Volscians were now his nation, and nothing would move him. At last, however, all the women of Rome came forth, headed by his mother Veturia and his wife Volumnia, each with a little child, and Veturia entreated and commanded her son in the most touching manner to change his purpose and cease to ruin his country, begging him, if he meant to destroy Rome, to begin by slaying her. She threw herself at his feet as she spoke, and his hard spirit gave way.

"Ah! mother, what is it you do?" he cried as he lifted her up. "Thou hast saved Rome, but lost thy son."

And so it proved, for when he had broken up his camp and returned to the Volscian territory till the senate should recall him as they proceeded, Tullus, angry and disappointed, stirred up a tumult, and he was killed by the people before he could be sent for to Rome. A temple to "Women's Good Speed" was raised on the spot where Veturia knelt to him. Another very proud patrician family was the Quinctian. The father, Lucius Quinctius, was called Cincinnatus, from his long flowing curls of hair. He was the ablest man among the Romans, but stern and grave, and his eldest son Kæso was charged by the tribunes with a murder and fled the country.

ROMAN CAMP

Soon after there was a great inroad of the Æqui and Volscians, and the Romans found themselves in great danger. They saw no one could save them but Cincinnatus, so they met in haste and chose him Dictator, though he was not present. Messengers were sent to his little farm on the Tiber, and there they found him holding the stilts of the plough. When they told their errand, he turned to his wife, who was helping him, and said, "Racilia, fetch me my toga;" then he washed his face and hands, and was saluted as Dictator. A boat was ready to take him to Rome, and as he landed, he was met by the four-and-twenty lictors belonging to the two consuls and escorted to his dwelling. In the morning he named as general of the cavalry Lucius Tarquitius, a brave old patrician who had become too poor even to keep a horse. Marching out at the head of all the men who could bear arms, he thoroughly routed the Æqui, and then resigned his dictatorship at the end of sixteen days. Nor would he accept any of the spoil, but went back to his plough, his only reward being that his son was forgiven and recalled from banishment.

PLOUGHING

These are the grand old stories that came down from old time, but how much is true no one can tell, and there is reason to think that, though the leaders like Cincinnatus and Coriolanus might be brave, the Romans were really pressed hard by the Volscians and Æqui, and lost a good deal of ground, though they were too proud to own it. No wonder, while the two orders of the state were always pulling different ways. However, the tribune Icilius succeeded in the year 454 in getting the Aventine Hill granted to the plebeians; and they had another champion called Lucius Sicinius Dentatus, who was so brave that he was called the Roman Achilles. He had received no less than forty-five wounds in different fights before he was fifty-eight years old, and had had fourteen civic crowns. For the Romans gave an oak-leaf wreath, which they called a civic crown, to a man who saved the life of a fellow-citizen, and a mural crown to him who first scaled the walls of a besieged city. And when a consul had gained a great victory, he had what was called a triumph. He was drawn in his chariot into the city, his victorious troops marching before him with their spears waving with laurel boughs, a wreath of laurel was on his head, his little children sat with him in the chariot, and the spoil of the enemy was carried along. All the people decked their houses and came forth rejoicing in holiday array, while he proceeded to the Capitol to sacrifice an ox to Jupiter there. His chief prisoners walked behind his car in chains, and at the moment of his sacrifice they were taken to a cell below the Capitol and there put to death, for the Roman was cruel in his joy. Nothing was more desired than such a triumph; but such was often the hatred between the plebeians and the patricians, that sometimes the plebeian army would stop short in the middle of a victorious campaign to hinder their consul from having a triumph. Even Sicinius is said once to have acted thus, and it began to be plain that Rome must fall if it continued to be thus divided against itself.

CHAPTER X.
THE DECEMVIRS.
B.C. 450.

The Romans began to see what mischiefs their quarrels did, and they agreed to send three of their best and wisest men to Greece to study the laws of Solon at Athens, and report whether any of them could be put in force at Rome.

To get the new code of laws which they brought home put into working order, it was agreed for the time to have no consuls, prætors, nor tribunes, but ten governors, perhaps in imitation of the nine Athenian archons. They were called Decemvirs (*decem*, ten; *vir*, a man), and at their head was Lucius Appius Claudius, the grandson of him who had killed himself to avoid being condemned for his harshness. At first they governed well, and a very good set of laws was drawn up, which the Romans called the Laws of the Ten Tables; but Appius soon began to give way to the pride of his nature, and made himself hated. There was a war with the Æqui, in which the Romans were beaten. Old Sicinius Dentatus said it was owing to bad management, and, as he had been in one hundred and twenty battles, everybody believed him. Thereupon Appius Claudius sent for him, begged for his advice, and asked him to join the army that he might assist the commanders. They received him warmly, and, when he advised them to move their camp, asked him to go and choose a place, and sent a guard with him of one hundred men. But these were really wretches instructed to kill him, and as soon as he was in a narrow rocky pass they set upon him. The brave old warrior set his back against a rock and fought so fiercely that he killed many, and the rest durst not come near him, but climbed up the rock and crushed him with stones rolled down on his head. Then they went back with a story that they had been attacked by the enemy, which was believed, till a party went out to bury the dead, and found there were only Roman corpses all lying round the crushed body of Sicinius, and that none were stripped of their armor or clothes. Then the true history was found out, but the Decemvirs sheltered the commanders, and would believe nothing against them.

Appius Claudius soon after did what horrified all honest men even more than this treachery to the brave old soldier. The Forum was not only the place of public assembly for state affairs, but the regular market-place, where there were stalls and booths for all the wares that Romans dealt in — meat stalls, wool shops, stalls where wine was sold in earthenware jars or leathern bottles, and even booths where reading and writing was taught to boys and girls, who would learn by tracing letters in the sand, and then by writing them with an iron pen on a waxen table in a frame, or with a reed upon parchment. The children of each family came escorted by a slave — the girls by their nurse, the boys by one called a pedagogue.

DEATH OF VIRGINIA.

Appius, when going to his judgment-seat across the Forum, saw at one of these schools a girl of fifteen reading her lesson. She was so lovely that he asked her nurse who she was, and heard that her name was Virginia, and that she was the daughter of an honorable plebeian and brave centurion named Virginius, who was absent with the army fighting with the Æqui, and that she was to marry a young man named Icilius as soon as the campaign was over. Appius would gladly have married her himself, but there was a patrician law against wedding plebeians, and he wickedly determined that if he could not have her for his wife he would have her for his slave.

There was one of his clients named Marcus Claudius, whom he paid to get up a story that Virginius' wife Numitoria, who was dead, had never had any child at all, but had bought a baby of one of his slaves and had deceived her husband with it, and thus that poor Virginia was really his slave. As the maiden was reading at her school, this wretch and a band of fellows like him seized upon her, declaring that she was his property, and that he would carry her off. There was a great uproar, and she was dragged as far as Appius' judgment-seat; but by that time her faithful nurse had called the poor girl's uncle Numitorius, who could answer for it that she was really his sister's child. But Appius would not listen to him, and all that he could gain was that judgment should not be given in the matter until Virginius should have been fetched from the camp.

Virginius had set out from the camp with Icilius before the messengers of Appius had reached the general with orders to stop him, and he came to the Forum leading his daughter by the hand, weeping, and attended by a great many ladies. Claudius brought his slave, who made false oath that she had sold her child to Numitoria; while, on the other hand, all the kindred of Virginius and his wife gave such proof of the contrary as any honest judge would have thought sufficient, but Appius chose to declare that the truth was with his client.

CHARIOT RACES.

There was a great murmur of all the people, but he frowned at them, and told them he knew of their meetings, and that there were soldiers in the Capitol ready to punish them, so they must stand back and not hinder a master from recovering his slave.

Virginius took his poor daughter in his arms as if to give her a last embrace, and drew her close to the stall of a butcher where lay a great knife. He wiped her tears, kissed her, and saying, "My own dear little girl, there is no way but this," he snatched up the knife and plunged it into her heart, then drawing it out he cried, "By this blood, Appius, I devote thy blood to the infernal gods."

He could not reach Appius, but the lictors could not seize him, and he mounted his horse and galloped back to the army, four hundred men following him, and he arrived still holding the knife. Every soldier who heard the story resolved no longer to bear with the Decemvirs, but to march back to the city at once and insist on the old government being restored. The Decemvir generals tried to stop them, but they only answered, "We are men with swords in our hands." At the same time there was such a tumult in the city, that Appius was forced to hide himself in his own house while Virginia's corpse was carried on a bier through the streets, and every one laid garlands, scarfs, and wreaths of their own hair upon it. When the troops arrived, they and the people joined in demanding that the Decemvirs should be given up to them to be burnt alive, and that the old magistrates should be restored. However, two patricians, Lucius Valerius and Marcus Horatius, were able so to arrange matters that the nine comparatively innocent Decemvirs were allowed to depose themselves, and Appius only was sent to prison, where he killed himself rather than face the trial that awaited him. The new code of laws, however, remained, but consuls, prætors, tribunes, and all the rest of the magistrates were restored, and in the year 445 a law was passed which enabled patricians and plebeians to intermarry.

CHAPTER XI.
CAMILLUS' BANISHMENT.
B.C. 390.

The wars with the Etruscans went on, and chiefly with the city of Veii, which stood on a hill twelve miles from Rome, and was altogether thirty years at war with it. At last the Romans made up their minds that, instead of going home every harvest-time to gather in their crops, they must watch the city constantly till they could take it, and thus, as the besiegers were unable to do their own work, pay was raised for them to enable them to get it done, and this was the beginning of paying armies.

ARROW MACHINE.

The siege of Veii lasted ten years, and during the last the Alban lake filled to an unusual height, although the summer was very dry. One of the Veian soldiers cried out to the Romans half in jest, "You will never take Veii till the Alban lake is dry." It turned out that there was an old tradition that Veii should fall when the lake was drained. On this the senate sent orders to have canals dug to carry the waters to the sea, and these still remain. Still Veii held out, and to finish the war a dictator was appointed, Marcus Furius Camillus, who chose for his second in command a man of one of the most virtuous families in Rome, as their surname testified, Publius Cornelius, called Scipio, or the Staff, because either he or one of his forefathers had been the staff of his father's old age. Camillus took the city by assault, with an immense quantity of spoil, which was divided among the soldiers.

Camillus in his pride took to himself at his triumph honors that had hitherto only been paid to the gods. He had his face painted with vermilion and his car drawn by milk-white horses. This shocked the people, and he gave greater offence by declaring that he had vowed a tenth part of the spoil to Apollo, but had forgotten it in the division of the plunder, and now must take it again. The soldiers would not consent, but lest the god should be angry with them, it was resolved to send a gold vase to his oracle at Delphi. All the women of Rome brought their jewels, and the senate rewarded them by a decree that funeral speeches might be made over their graves as over those of men, and likewise that they might be driven in chariots to the public games.

Camillus commanded in another war with the Falisci, also an Etruscan race, and laid siege to their city. The sons of almost all the chief families were in charge of a sort of schoolmaster, who taught them both reading and all kinds of exercises. One day this man, pretending to take the boys out walking, led them all into the enemy's camp, to the tent of Camillus, where he told that he brought them all, and with them the place, since the Romans had only to threaten their lives to make their fathers deliver up the city. Camillus, however, was so shocked at such perfidy, that he immediately bade the lictors strip the fellow instantly, and give the boys rods with which to scourge him back into the town. Their fathers were so grateful that they made peace at once, and about the same time the Æqui were also conquered; and the commons and open lands belonging to Veii being divided, so that each Roman freeman had six acres, the plebeians were contented for the time.

SIEGE MACHINE

The truth seems to have been that these Etruscan nations were weakened by a great new nation coming on them from the North. They were what the Romans called Galli or Gauls, one of the great races of the old stock which has always been finding its way westward into Europe, and they had their home north of the Alps, but they were always pressing on and on, and had long since made settlements in northern Italy. They were in clans, each obedient to one chief as a father, and joining together in one brotherhood. They had lands to which whole families had a common right, and when their numbers outgrew what the land could maintain, the bolder ones would set off with their wives, children, and cattle to find new homes. The Greeks and Romans themselves had begun first in the same way, and their tribes, and the claims of all to the common land, were the remains of the old way; but they had been settled in cities so long that this had been forgotten, and they were very different people from the wild men who spoke what we call Welsh, and wore checked tartan trews and plaids, with gold collars round their necks, round shields, huge broadswords, and their red or black hair long and shaggy. The Romans knew little or nothing about what passed beyond their own Apennines, and went on with their own quarrels. Camillus was accused of having taken more than his proper share of the spoil of Veii, in especial a brass door from a temple. His friends offered to pay any fine that might be laid on him, but he was too proud to stand his trial, and chose rather to leave Rome. As he passed the gates, he turned round and called upon the gods to bring Rome to speedy repentance for having driven him away.

Even then the Gauls were in the midst of a war with Clusium, the city of Porsena, and the inhabitants sent to beg the help of the Romans, and the senate sent three young brothers of the Fabian family to try to arrange matters. They met the Gaulish Bran or chief, whom Latin authors call Brennus, and asked him what was his quarrel with Clusium or his right to any part of Etruria. Brennus answered that his right was his sword, and that all things belonged to the brave, and that his quarrel with the men of Clusium was, that though they had more land than they could till, they would not yield him any. As to the Romans, they had robbed their neighbors already, and had no right to find fault.

This put the Fabian brothers in a rage, and they forgot the caution of their family, as well as those rules of all nations which forbid an ambassador to fight, and also forbid his person to be touched by the enemy; and when the men of Clusium made an attack on the Gauls they joined in the attack, and Quintus, the eldest brother, slew one of the chiefs. Brennus, wild as he was, knew these laws of nations, and in great anger broke up his siege of Clusium, and, marching towards Rome, demanded that the Fabii should be given up to him. Instead of this, the Romans made them all three military tribunes, and as the Gauls came nearer the whole army marched out to meet them in such haste that they did not wait to sacrifice to the gods nor consult the omens. The tribunes were all young and hot-headed, and they despised the Gauls; so out they went to attack them on the banks of the Allia, only seven and a-half miles from Rome. A most terrible defeat they had; many fell in the field, many were killed in the flight, others were drowned in trying to swim the Tiber, others scattered to Veii and the other cities, and a few, horror-stricken and wet through, rushed into Rome with the sad tidings. There were not men enough left to defend the walls! The enemy would instantly be upon them! The only place strong enough to keep them out was the Capitol, and that would only hold a few people within it! So there was nothing for it but flight. The braver, stronger men shut themselves up in the Capitol; all the rest, with the women and children, put their most precious goods into carts and left the city. The Vestal Virgins carried the sacred fire, and were plodding along in the heat, when a plebeian named Albinus saw their state, helped them into his cart, and took them to the city of Cumæ, where they found shelter in a temple. And so Rome was left to the enemy.

CHAPTER XII.
THE SACK OF ROME.
B.C. 390.

Rome was left to the enemy, except for the small garrison in the Capitol and for eighty of the senators, men too old to flee, who devoted themselves to the gods to save the rest, and, arraying themselves in their robes — some as former consuls, some as priests, some as generals — sat down with their ivory staves in their hands, in their chairs of state in the Forum, to await the enemy.

RUINS OF THE FORUM AT ROME.

In burst the savage Gauls, roaming all over the city till they came to the Forum, where they stood amazed and awe-struck at the sight of the eighty grand old men motionless in their chairs. At first they looked at the strange, calm figures as if they were the gods of the place, until one Gaul, as if desirous of knowing whether they were flesh and blood or not, stroked the beard of the nearest. The senator, esteeming this an insult, struck the man on the face with his staff, and this was the sign for the slaughter of them all.

Then the Gauls began to plunder every house, dragging out and killing the few inhabitants they found there; feasting, revelling, and piling up riches to carry away; burning and overthrowing the houses. Day after day the little garrison in the Capitol saw the sight, and wondered if their stock of food would hold out till the Gauls should go away or till their friends should come to their relief. Yet when the day came round for the sacrifice to the ancestor of one of these beleaguered men, he boldly went forth to the altar of his own ruined house on the Quirinal Hill, and made his offering to his forefathers, nor did one Gaul venture to touch him, seeing that he was performing a religious rite.

The escaped Romans had rested at Ardea, where they found Camillus, and were by him formed into an army, but he would not take the generalship without authority from what was left of the Senate, and that was shut up in the Capitol in the midst of the Gauls. A brave man, however, named Pontius Cominius, declared that he could make his way through the Gauls by night, and climb up the Capitol and down again by a precipice which they did not watch because they thought no one could mount it, and that he would bring back the orders of the Senate. He swam the Tiber by the help of corks, landed at night in ruined Rome among the sleeping enemy, and climbed up the rock, bringing hope at last to the worn-out and nearly starving garrison. Quickly they met, recalled the sentence of banishment against Camillus, and named him Dictator. Pontius, having rested in the meantime, slid down the rock and made his way back to Ardea safely; but the broken twigs and torn ivy on the rock showed the Gauls that it had been scaled, and they resolved that where man had gone man could go. So Brennus told off the most surefooted mountaineers he could find, and at night, two and two, they crept up the crag, so silently that no alarm was given, till just as they came to the top, some geese that were kept as sacred to Juno, and for that reason had been spared in spite of the scarcity, began to scream and cackle, and thus brought to the spot a brave officer called Marcus Manlius, who found two Gauls in the act of setting foot on the level ground on the top. With a sweep of his sword he struck off the hand of one, and with his buckler smote the other on the head, tumbling them both headlong down, knocking down their fellows in their flight, and the Capitol was saved.

By way of reward every Roman soldier brought Manlius a few grains of the corn he received from the common stock and a few drops of wine, while the tribune who was on guard that night was thrown from the rock.

Foiled thus, and with great numbers of his men dying from the fever that always prevailed in Rome in summer, Brennus thought of retreating, and offered to leave Rome if the garrison in the Capitol would pay him a thousand pounds' weight of gold. There was treasure enough in the temples to do this, and as they could not tell what Camillus was about, nor if Pontius had reached him safely, and they were on the point of being starved, they consented. The gold was brought to the place appointed by the Gauls, and when the weights proved not to be equal to the amount that the Romans had with them, Brennus resolved to have all, put his sword into the other scale, saying, "Væ victis" — "Woe to the conquered." But at that moment there was a noise outside — Camillus was come. The Gauls were cut down and slain among the ruins, those who fled were killed by the people in the country as they wandered in the fields, and not one returned to tell the tale. So the ransom of the Capitol was rescued, and was laid up by Camillus in the vaults as a reserve for future danger.

This was the Roman story, but their best historians say that it is made better for Rome than is quite the truth, for that the Capitol was really conquered, and the Gauls helped themselves to whatever they chose and went off with it, though sickness and weariness made them afterwards disperse, so that they were mostly cut off by the country people.

Every old record had been lost and destroyed, so that, before this, Roman history can only be hearsay, derived from what the survivors recollected; and the whole of the buildings, temples, senate-house, and dwellings lay in ruins. Some of the citizens wished to change the site of the city to Veii; but Camillus, who was Dictator, was resolved to hold fast by the hearths of their fathers, and while the debate was going on in the ruins of the senate-house a troop of soldiers were marching in, and the centurion was heard calling out, "Plant your ensign here; this is a good place to stay in." "A happy omen," cried one of the senators; "I adore the gods who gave it." So it was settled to rebuild the city, and in digging among the ruins there were found the golden rod of Romulus, the brazen tables on which the Laws of the Twelve Tables were engraved, and other brasses with records of treaties with other nations. Fabius was accused of having done all the harm by having broken the law of nations, but he was spared at the entreaty of his friends. Manlius was surnamed Capitolinus, and had a house granted him on the Capitol; and Camillus when he laid down his dictatorship, was saluted as like Romulus — another founder of Rome.

The new buildings were larger and more ornamented than the old ones; but the lines of the old underground drains, built in the mighty Etruscan fashion by the elder Tarquin as it was said, were not followed, and this tended to render Rome more unhealthy, so that few of her richer citizens lived there in summer or autumn, but went out to country houses on the hills.

ENTRY OF THE FORUM ROMANUM BY THE VIA SACRA

CHAPTER XIII.
THE PLEBEIAN CONSULATE.
B.C. 367.

All the old enemies of Rome attacked her again when she was weak and rising out of her ruins, but Camillus had wisely persuaded the Romans to add the people of Veii, Capena, and Falerii to the number of their citizens, making four more tribes; and this addition to their numbers helped them beat off their foes.

But this enlarged the number of the plebeians, and enabled them to make their claims more heard. Moreover, the old quarrel between poor and rich, debtor and creditor, broke out again. Those who had saved their treasure in the time of the sack had made loans to those who had lost to enable them to build their houses and stock their farms again, and after a time they called loudly for payment, and when it was not forthcoming had the debtors seized to be sold as slaves. Camillus himself was one of the hardest creditors of all, and the barracks where slaves were placed to be sold were full of citizens.

COSTUMES.

Marcus Manlius Capitolinus was full of pity, and raised money to redeem four hundred of them, trying with all his might to get the law changed and to save the rest; but the rich men and the patricians thought he acted only out of jealousy of Camillus, and to get up a party for himself. They said he was raising a sedition, and Publius Cornelius Cossus was named Dictator to put it down. Manlius was seized and put into chains, but released again. At last the rich men bought over two of the tribunes to accuse him of wanting to make himself a king, and this hated title turned all the people against their friend, so that the general cry sentenced him to be cast down from the top of the Tarpeian rock; his house on the Capitol was overthrown, and his family declared that no son of their house should ever again bear the name of Manlius.

COSTUME.

Yet the plebeians were making their way, and at last succeeded in gaining the plebeian magistracies and equal honors with the patricians. A curious story is told of the cause of the last effort which gained the day. A patrician named Fabius Ambustus had two daughters, one of whom he gave in marriage to Servius Sulpicius, a patrician and military tribune, the other to Licinius Stolo. One day, when Stolo's wife was visiting her sister, there was a great noise and thundering at the gates which frightened her, until the other Fabii said it was only her husband coming home from the Forum attended by his lictors and clients, laughing at her ignorance and alarm, until a whole troop of the clients came in to pay their court to the tribune's wife.

Stolo's wife went home angry and vexed, and reproached her husband and her father for not having made her equal with her sister, and so wrought on them that they put themselves at the head of the movement in favor of the plebeians; and Licinius and another young plebeian named Lucius Sextius, being elected year after year tribunes of the people, went on every time saying *Veto* to whatever was proposed by anybody, and giving out that they should go on doing so till three measures were carried — viz., that interest on debt should not be demanded; that no citizen should possess more than three hundred and twenty acres of the public land, or feed more than a certain quantity of cattle on the public pastures; and, lastly, that one of the two consuls should always be a plebeian.

They went on for eight years, always elected by the people and always stopping everything. At last there was another inroad of the Gauls expected, and Camillus, though eighty years old, was for the fifth time chosen Dictator, and gained a great victory upon the banks of the Anio. The Senate begged him to continue Dictator till he could set their affairs to rights, and he vowed to build a temple to Concord if he could succeed. He saw indeed that it was time to yield, and persuaded the Senate to think so; so that at last, in the year 367, Sextius was elected consul, together with a patrician, Æmilius. Even then the Senate would not receive Sextius till he was introduced by Camillus. From this time the patricians and plebeians were on an equal footing as far as regarded the magistracies, but the priesthood could belong only to the patricians. Camillus lived to a great age, and was honored as having three times saved his country. He died at last of a terrible pestilence which raged in Rome in the year 365.

The priests recommended that they should invite the players from Etruria to perform a drama in honor of the feats of the gods, and this was the beginning of play-acting in Rome.

Not long after there yawned a terrible chasm in the Forum, most likely from an earthquake, but nothing seemed to fill it up, and the priests and augurs consulted their oracles about it. These made answer that it would only close on receiving of what was most precious. Gold and jewels were thrown in, but it still seemed bottomless, and at last the augurs declared that it was courage that was the most precious thing in Rome. Thereupon a patrician youth named Marcus Curtius decked himself in his choicest robes, put on his armor, took his shield, sword, and spear, mounted his horse, and leapt headlong into the gulf, thus giving it the most precious of all things, courage and self-devotion. After this one story says it closed of itself, another that it became easy to fill it up with earth.

The Romans thought that such a sacrifice must please the gods and bring them success in their battles; but in the war with the Hernici that was now being waged the plebeian consul was killed, and no doubt there was much difficulty in getting the patricians to obey a plebeian properly, for in the course of the next twenty years it was necessary fourteen times to appoint a Dictator for the defence of the state, so that it is plain there must have been many alarms and much difficulty in enforcing discipline; but, on the whole, success was with Rome, and the neighboring tribes grew weaker.

CURTIUS LEAPING INTO THE GULF. (From a Bas-Relief.)

CHAPTER XIV.
THE DEVOTION OF DECIUS.
B.C. 357

Other tribes of the Gauls did not fail to come again and make fresh inroads on the valleys of the Tiber and Anio. Whenever they came, instead of choosing men from the tribes to form an army, as in a war with their neighbors, all the fighting men of the nation turned out to oppose them, generally under a Dictator.

In one of these wars the Gauls came within three miles of Rome, and the two hosts were encamped on the banks of the Anio, with a bridge between them. Along this bridge strutted an enormous Gallic chief, much taller than any of the Romans, boasting himself, and calling on any one of them to come out and fight with him. Again it was a Manlius who distinguished himself. Titus, a young man of that family, begged the Dictator's permission to accept the challenge, and, having gained it, he changed his round knight's shield for the square one of the foot soldiers, and with his short sword came forward on the bridge. The Gaul made a sweep at him with his broadsword, but, slipping within the guard, Manlius stabbed the giant in two places, and as he fell cut off his head, and took the torc, or broad twisted gold collar that was the mark of all Gallic chieftains. Thence the brave youth was called Titus Manlius Torquatus — a surname to make up for that of Capitolinus, which had never been used again.

The next time the Gauls came, Marcus Valerius, a descendant of the old hero Publicola, was consul, and gained a great victory. It was said that in the midst of the fight a monstrous raven appeared flying over his head, resting now and then on his helmet, but generally pecking at the eyes of the Gauls and flapping its wings in their faces, so that they fled discomfited. Thence he was called Corvus or Corvinus.

THE APENNINES.

The Gauls never again came in such force, but a new enemy came against them, namely, the Samnites, a people who dwelt to the south of them. They were of Italian blood, mountaineers of the Southern Apennines, not unlike the Romans in habits, language, and training, and the staunchest enemies they had yet encountered. The war began from an entreaty from the people of Campania to the Romans to defend them from the attacks of the Samnites. For the Campanians, living in the rich plains, whose name is still unchanged, were an idle, languid people, whom the stout men of Samnium could easily overcome. The Romans took their part, and Valerius Corvus gained a victory at Mount Gaurus; but the other consul, Cornelius Cossus, fell into danger, having marched foolishly into a forest, shut in by mountains, and with only one way out through a deep valley, which was guarded by the Samnites. In this almost hopeless danger one of the military tribunes, Publius Decius Mus, discovered a little hill above the enemy's camp, and asked leave to lead a small body of men to seize it, since he would be likely thus to draw off the Samnites, and while they were destroying him, as he fully expected, the Romans could get out of the valley. Hidden by the wood, he gained the hill, and there the Samnites saw him, to their great amazement; and while they were considering whether to attack him, the other Romans were able to march out of the valley. Finding he was not attacked, Decius set guards, and, when night came on, marched down again as quietly as possible to join the army, who were now on the other side of the Samnite camp. Through the midst of this he and his little camp went without alarm, until, about half-way across, one Roman struck his foot against a shield. The noise awoke the Samnites, but Decius caused his men to give a great shout, and this, in the darkness, so confused the enemy that they missed the little body of Romans, who safely gained their own camp. Decius cut short the thanks and joy of the consul by advising him to fall at once on the Samnite camp in its dismay, and this was done; the Samnites were entirely routed, 30,000 killed, and their camp taken. Decius received for his reward a hundred oxen, a white bull with gilded horns, and three crowns — one of gold for courage, one of oak for having saved the lives of his fellow-citizens, and one of grass for having taken the enemy's camp — while all his men were for life to receive a double allowance of corn. Decius offered up the white bull in sacrifice to Mars, and gave the oxen to the companions of his glory.

Afterwards Valerius routed the Samnites again, and his troops brought in 120 standards and 40,000 shields which they had picked up, having been thrown away by the enemy in their flight.

Peace was made for the time; but the Latins, now in alliance with Rome, began to make war on the Samnites. They complained, and the Romans feeling bound to take their part, a great Latin war began. Manlius Torquatus and Decius Mus, the two greatest heroes of Rome, were consuls. As the Latins and Romans were alike in dress, arms, and language, in order to prevent taking friend for foe, strict orders were given that no one should attack a Latin without orders, or go out of his rank, on pain of death. A Latin champion came out boasting, as the two armies lay beneath Mount Vesuvius, then a fair vine-clad hill showing no flame. Young Manlius remembering his father's fame, darted out, fought hand to hand with the Latin, slew him, and brought home his spoils to his father's feet. He had forgotten that his father had only fought after permission was given. The elder Manlius received him with stern grief. He had broken the law of discipline, and he must die. His head was struck off amid the grief and anger of the army. The battle was bravely fought, but it went against the Romans at first. Then Decius, recollecting a vision which had declared that a consul must devote himself for his country, called on Valerius, the Pontifex Maximus, to dedicate him. He took off his armor, put on his purple toga, covered his head with a veil, and standing on a spear, repeated the words of consecration after Valerius, then mounted his horse and rode in among the Latins. They at first made way, but presently closed in and overpowered him with a shower of darts; and thus he gave for his country the life he had once offered for it.

The victory was won, and was so followed up that the Latins were forced to yield to Rome. Some of the cities retained their own laws and magistrates, but others had Romans with their families settled in them, and were called colonies, while the Latin people themselves became Roman citizens in everything but the power of becoming magistrates or voting for them, being, in fact, very much what the earliest plebeians had been before they acquired any rights.

CHAPTER XV.
THE SAMNITE WARS.

In the year 332, just when Alexander the Great was making his conquests in the East, his uncle Alexander, king of Epirus, brother to his mother Olympius, came to Italy, where there were so many Grecian citizens south of the Samnites that the foot of Italy was called Magna Græcia, or Greater Greece. He attacked the Samnites, and the Romans were not sorry to see them weakened, and made an alliance with him. He stayed in Italy about six years, and was then killed.

To overthrow the Samnites was the great object of Rome at this time, and for this purpose they offered their protection and alliance to all the cities that stood in dread of that people. One of the cities was founded by men from the isle of Euboea, who called it Neapolis, or the New City, to distinguish it from the old town near at hand, which they called Palæopolis, or the Old City. The elder city held out against the Romans, but was easily overpowered, while the new one submitted to Rome; but these southern people were very shallow and fickle, and little to be depended on, as they often changed sides between the Romans and Samnites. In the midst of the siege of Palæopolis, the year of the consulate came to an end, but the Senate, while causing two consuls as usual to be elected, at home, would not recall Publilius Philo from the siege, and therefore appointed him proconsul there. This was in 326, and was the beginning of the custom of sending the ex-consul as proconsul to command the armies or govern the provinces at a distance from home.

In 320, the consul falling sick, a dictator was appointed, Lucius Papirius Cursor, one of the most stern and severe men in Rome. He was obliged by some religious ceremony to return to Rome for a time, and he forbade his lieutenant, Quintus Fabius Rullianus, to venture a battle in his absence.

COMBAT BETWEEN A MIRMILLO AND A SAMNITE.

COMBAT BETWEEN A LIGHT-ARMED GLADIATOR AND A SAMNITE.

But so good an opportunity offered that Fabius attacked the enemy, beat them, and killed 20,000 men. Then selfishly unwilling to have the spoils he had won carried in the dictator's triumph, he burnt them all. Papirius arrived in great anger, and sentenced him to death for his disobedience; but while the lictors were stripping him, he contrived to escape from their hands among the soldiers, who closed on him, so that he was able to get to Rome, where his father called the Senate together, and they showed themselves so resolved to save his life that Papirius was forced to pardon him, though not without reproaching the Romans for having fallen from the stern justice of Brutus and Manlius.

Two years later the two consuls, Titus Veturius and Spurius Posthumius, were marching into Campania, when the Samnite commander, Pontius Herennius, sent forth people disguised as shepherds to entice them into a narrow mountain pass near the city of Candium, shut in by thick woods, leading into a hollow curved valley, with thick brushwood on all sides, and only one way out, which the Samnites blocked up with trunks of trees. As soon as the Romans were within this place the other end was blocked in the same way, and thus they were all closed up at the mercy of their enemies.

What was to be done with them? asked the Samnites; and they went to consult old Herennius, the father of Pontius, the wisest man in the nation. "Open the way and let them all go free," he said.

"What! without gaining any advantage?"

"Then kill them all."

He was asked to explain such extraordinary advice. He said that to release them generously would be to make them friends and allies for ever; but if the war was to go on, the best thing for Samnium would be to destroy such a number of enemies at a blow. But the Samnites could not resolve upon either plan; so they took a middle course, the worst of all, since it only made the Romans furious without weakening them. They were made to take off all their armor and lay down their weapons, and thus to pass out under the yoke, namely, three spears set up like a doorway. The consuls, after agreeing to a disgraceful peace, had to go first, wearing only their undermost garment, then all the rest, two and two, and if any one of them gave an angry look, he was immediately knocked down and killed. They went on in silence into Campania, where, when night came on, they all threw themselves, half-naked, silent, and hungry upon the grass. The people of Capua came out to help them, and brought them food and clothing, trying to do them all honor and comfort them, but they would neither look up nor speak. And thus they went on to Rome, where everybody had put on mourning, and all the ladies went without their jewels, and the shops in the Forum were closed. The unhappy men stole into their houses at night one by one, and the consuls would not resume their office, but two were appointed to serve instead for the rest of the year.

ANCIENT ROME.

Revenge was all that was thought of, but the difficulty was the peace to which the consuls had sworn. Posthumius said that if it was disavowed by the Senate, he, who had been driven to make it, must be given back to the Samnites. So, with his hands tied, he was taken back to the Samnite camp by a herald and delivered over; but at that moment Posthumius gave the herald a kick, crying out, "I am now a Samnite, and have insulted you, a Roman herald. This is a just cause of war." Pontius and the Samnites were very angry, and they said it was an unworthy trick; but they did not prevent Posthumius from going safely back to the Romans, who considered him to have quite retrieved his honor.

A battle was fought, in which Pontius and 7000 men were forced to lay down their arms and pass under the yoke in their turn. The struggle between these two fierce nations lasted altogether seventy years, and the Romans had many defeats. They had other wars at the same time. They never subdued Etruria, and in the battle of Sentinum, fought with the Gauls, the consul Decius Mus, devoted himself exactly as his father had done at Vesuvius, and by his death won the victory.

The Samnite wars may be considered as ending in 290, when the chief general of Samnium, Pontius Telesimus, was made prisoner and put to death at Rome. The lands in the open country were quite subdued, but many Samnites still lived in the fastnesses of the Apennines in the south, which have ever since been the haunt of wild untamed men.

CHAPTER XVI.
THE WAR WITH PYRRHUS.
B.C. 280-271.

In the Grecian History you remember that Pyrrhus, king of Epirus, the townsman of Alexander the Great, made an expedition to Italy. This was the way it came about. The city of Tarentum was a Spartan colony at the head of the gulf that bears its name. It was as proud as its parent, but had lost all the grave sternness of manners, and was as idle and fickle as the other places in that languid climate. The Tarentines first maltreated some Roman ships which put into their gulf, and then insulted the ambassador who was sent to complain. Then when the terrible Romans were found to be really coming to revenge their honor, the Tarentines took fright, and sent to beg Pyrrhus to come to their aid.

He readily accepted the invitation, and coming to Italy with 28,000 men and twenty elephants, hoped to conquer the whole country; but he found the Tarentines not to be trusted, and soon weary of entertaining him, while they could not keep their promises of aid from the other Greeks of Italy.

The Romans marched against him, and there was a great battle on the banks of the river Siris, where the fighting was very hard, but when the elephants charged the Romans broke and fled, and were only saved by nightfall from being entirely destroyed.

So great, however, had been Pyrrhus' loss that he said, "Such another victory, and I shall have to go back alone to Epirus."

He thought he had better treat with the Romans, and sent his favorite counsellor Kineas to offer to make peace, provided the Romans would promise safety to his Italian allies, and presents were sent to the senators and their wives to induce them to listen favorably.

PYRRHUS.

People in ancient Greece expected such gifts to back a suit; but Kineas found that nobody in Rome would hear of being bribed, though many were not unwilling to make peace. Blind old Appius Claudius, who had often been consul, caused himself to be led into the Senate to oppose it, for it was hard to his pride to make peace as defeated men. Kineas was much struck with Rome, where he found a state of things like the best days of Greece, and, going back to his master, told him that the senate-house was like a temple, and those who sat there like an assembly of kings, and that he feared they were fighting with the Hydra of Lerna, for as soon as they had destroyed one Roman army another had sprung up in its place.

However, the Romans wanted to treat about the prisoners Pyrrhus had taken, and they sent Caius Fabricius to the Greek camp for the purpose. Kineas reported him to be a man of no wealth, but esteemed as a good soldier and an honest man. Pyrrhus tried to make him take large presents, but nothing would Fabricius touch; and then, in the hope of alarming him, in the middle of a conversation the hangings of one side of the tent suddenly fell, and disclosed the biggest of all the elephants, who waved his trunk over Fabricius and trumpeted frightfully. The Roman quietly turned round and smiled as he said to the king, "I am no more moved by your gold than by your great beast."

ROMAN ORATOR.

At supper there was a conversation on Greek philosophy, of which the Romans as yet knew nothing. When the doctrine of

Epicurus was mentioned, that man's life was given to be spent in the pursuit of joy, Fabricius greatly amused the company by crying out, "O Hercules! grant that the Greeks may be heartily of this mind so long as we have to fight with them."

Pyrrhus even tried to persuade Fabricius to enter his service, but the answer was, "Sir. I advise you not; for if your people once tasted of my rule, they would all desire me to govern them instead of you." Pyrrhus consented to let the prisoners go home, but, if no peace were made, they were to return again as soon as the Saturnalia were over; and this was faithfully done. Fabricius was consul the next year, and thus received a letter from Pyrrhus' physician, offering for a reward to rid the Romans of his master by poison. The two consuls sent it to the king with the following letter: — "Caius Fabricius and Quintus Æmilius, consuls, to Pyrrhus, king, greeting. You choose your friends and foes badly. This letter will show that you make war with honest men and trust rogues and knaves. We tell you, not to win your favor, but lest your ruin might bring on the reproach of ending the war by treachery instead of force."

Pyrrhus made enquiry, put the physician to death, and by way of acknowledgment released the captives, trying again to make peace; but the Romans would accept no terms save that he should give up the Tarentines and go back in the same ships. A battle was fought in the wood of Asculum. Decius Mus declared he would devote himself like his father and grandfather; but Pyrrhus heard of this, and sent word that he had given orders that Decius should not be killed, but taken alive and scourged; and this prevented him. The Romans were again forced back by the might of the elephants, but not till night fell on them. Pyrrhus had been wounded, and hosts of Greeks had fallen, among them many of Pyrrhus' chief friends.

He then went to Sicily, on an invitation from the Greeks settled there, to defend them from the Carthaginians; but finding them as little satisfactory as the Italian Greeks, he suddenly came back to Tarentum. This time one of the consuls was Marcus Curius — called Dentatus, because he had been born with teeth in his mouth — a stout, plain old Roman, very stern, for when he levied troops against Pyrrhus, the first man who refused to serve was punished by having his property seized and sold. He then marched southward, and at Beneventum at length entirely defeated Pyrrhus, and took four of his elephants. Pyrrhus was obliged to return to Epirus, and the Roman steadiness had won the day after nine years.

Dentatus had the grandest triumph that had ever been known at Rome, with the elephants walking in the procession, the first that the Romans had ever seen. All the spoil was given up to the commonwealth; and when, some time after, it was asserted that he had taken some for himself, it turned out that he had only kept one old wooden vessel, which he used in sacrificing to the gods.

The Greeks of Southern Italy had behaved very ill to Pyrrhus and turned against him. The Romans found them so fickle and troublesome that they were all reduced in one little war after another. The Tarentines had to surrender and lose their walls and their fleet, and so had the people of Sybaris, who have become a proverb for idleness, for they were so lazy that they were said to have killed all their crowing-birds for waking them too early in the morning. All the peninsula of Italy now belonged to Rome, and great roads were made of paved stones connecting them with it, many of which remain to this day, even the first of all, called the Appian Way, from Rome to Capua, which was made under the direction of the censor Appius Claudius, during the Samnite war.

CHAPTER XVII.
THE FIRST PUNIC WAR.
264-240.

We are now come to the time when Rome became mixed up in wars with nations beyond Italy. There was a great settlement of the Phoenicians, the merchants of the old world, at Carthage, on the northern coast of Africa, the same place at which Virgil afterwards described Æneas as spending so much time. Dido, the queen who was said to have founded Carthage when fleeing from her wicked brother-in-law at Tyre, is thought to have been an old goddess, and the religion and manners of the Carthaginians were thoroughly Phoenician, or, as the Romans called them, Punic. They had no king, but a Senate, and therewith rulers called by the name that is translated as judges in the Bible; and they did not love war, only trade, and spread out their settlements for this purpose all over the coast of the Mediterranean, from Spain to the Black Sea, wherever a country had mines, wool, dyes, spices, or men to trade with; and their sailors were the boldest to be found anywhere, and were the only ones who had passed beyond the Pillars of Hercules, namely, the Straits of Gibraltar, in the Atlantic Ocean. They built handsome cities, and country houses with farms and gardens round them, and had all tokens of wealth and luxury — ivory, jewels, and spices from India, pearls from the Persian Gulf, gold from Spain, silver from the Balearic Isles, tin from the Scilly Isles, amber from the Baltic; and they had forts to protect their settlements. They generally hired the men of the countries, where they settled, to fight their battles, sometimes under hired Greek captains, but often under generals of their own.

The first place where they did not have everything their own way was Sicily. The old inhabitants of the island were called Sicels, a rough people; but besides these there were a great number of Greek settlements, also of Carthaginian ones, and these two hated one another.

ROMAN SHIP.

The Carthaginians tried to overthrow the Greeks, and Pyrrhus, by coming to help his countrymen, only made them more bitter against one another. When he went away he exclaimed, "What an arena we leave for the Romans and Carthaginians to contend upon!" so sure was he that these two great nations must soon fight out the struggle for power.

The beginning of the struggle was, however, brought on by another cause. Messina, the place founded long ago by the brave exiles of Messene, when the Spartans had conquered their state, had been seized by a troop of Mamertines, fierce Italians from Mamertum; and these, on being threatened by Xiero, king of Syracuse, sent to offer to become subjects to the Romans, thus giving them the command of the port which secured the entrance of the island. The Senate had great scruples about accepting the offer, and supporting a set of mere robbers; but the two consuls and all the people could not withstand the temptation, and it was resolved to assist the Mamertines. Thus began what was called the First Punic War. The difficulty was, however, want of ships. The Romans had none of their own, and though they collected a few from their Greek allies in Italy, it was not in time to prevent some of the Mamertines from surrendering the citadel to Xanno, the Carthaginian general, who thought himself secure, and came down to treat with the Roman tribune Claudius, haughtily bidding the Romans no more to try to meddle with the sea, for they should not be allowed so much as to wash their hands in it. Claudius, angered at this, treacherously laid hands on Xanno, and he agreed to give up the castle on being set free; but he had better have remained a prisoner, for the Carthaginians punished him with crucifixion, and besieged Messina, but in vain.

The Romans felt that a fleet was necessary, and set to work to build war galleys on the pattern of a Carthaginian one which had been wrecked upon their coast. While a hundred ships were building, oarsmen were trained to row on dry land, and in two months the fleet put to sea. Knowing that there was no chance of being able to fight according to the regular rules of running the beaks of their galleys into the sides of those of their enemies, they devised new plans of letting heavy weights descend on the ships of the opposite fleet, and then of letting drawbridges down by which to board them. The Carthaginians, surprised and dismayed, when thus attacked off Mylæ by the consul Duilius, were beaten and chased to Sardinia, where their unhappy commander was nailed to a cross by his own soldiers; while Duilius not only received in Rome a grand triumph for his first naval victory, but it was decreed that he should never go out into the city at night without a procession of torch-bearers.

The Romans now made up their minds to send an expedition to attack the Carthaginian power not only in Sicily but in Africa, and this was placed under the command of a sturdy plebeian consul, Marcus Attilius Regulus. He fought a great battle with the Carthaginian fleet on his way, and he had even more difficulty with his troops, who greatly dreaded the landing in Africa as a place of unknown terror. He landed, however, at some distance from the city, and did not at once advance on it. When he did, according to the story current at Rome, he encountered on the banks of the River Bagrada an enormous serpent, whose poisonous breath killed all who approached it, and on whose scales darts had no effect. At last the machines for throwing huge stones against city walls were used against it; its backbone was broken, and it was at last killed, and its skin sent to Rome.

The Romans met other enemies, whom they defeated, and gained much plunder. The Senate, understanding that the Carthaginians were cooped up within their walls, recalled half the army. Regulus wished much to return, as the slave who tilled his little farm had run away with his plough, and his wife was in distress; but he was so valuable that he could not be recalled, and he remained and soon took Tunis. The Carthaginians tried to win their gods' favor back by offering horrid human sacrifices to Moloch and Baal, and then hired a Spartan general named Xanthippus, who defeated the Romans, chiefly by means of the elephants, and made Regulus prisoner. The Romans, who hated the Carthaginians so much as to believe them capable of any wickedness, declared that in their jealousy of Xanthippus' victory, they sent him home to Greece in a vessel so arranged as to founder at sea.

However, the Romans, after several disasters in Sicily, gained a great victory near Panormus, capturing one hundred elephants, which were brought to Rome to be hunted by the people that they might lose their fear of them. The Carthaginians were weakened enough to desire peace, and they sent Regulus to propose it, making him swear to return if he did not succeed. He came to the outskirts of the city, but would not enter. He said he was no Roman proconsul, but the slave of Carthage. However, the Senate came out to hear him, and he gave the message, but added that the Romans ought not to accept these terms, but to stand out for much better ones, giving such reasons that the whole people was persuaded. He was entreated to remain and not meet the angry men of Carthage; but nothing would persuade him to break his word, and he went back.

ROMAN ORDER OF BATTLE.

The Romans told dreadful stories of the treatment he met with — how his eyelids were cut off and he was put in the sunshine, and at last he was nailed up in a barrel lined with spikes and rolled down hill. Some say that this was mere report, and that Carthaginian prisoners at Rome were as savagely treated; but at any rate the constancy of Regulus has always been a proverb.

The war went on, and one of the proud Claudius family was in command at Trepanum, in Sicily, when the enemy's fleet came in sight. Before a battle the Romans always consulted the sacred fowls that were carried with the army. Claudius was told that their augury was against a battle — they would not eat. "Then let them drink," he cried, and threw them into the sea. His impiety, as all felt it, was punished by an utter defeat, and he killed himself to avoid an enquiry. The war went on by land and sea all over and around Sicily, till at the end of twenty-four years peace was made, just after another great sea-fight, in which Rome had the victory. She made the Carthaginians give up all they held in Sicily, restore their prisoners, make a large payment, and altogether humble their claims; thus beginning a most bitter hatred towards the conquerors, who as greatly hated and despised them. Thus ended the First Punic War.

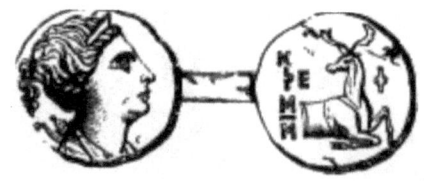

CHAPTER XVIII.
CONQUEST OF CISALPINE GAUL.
240-219.

After the end of the Punic war, Carthage fell into trouble with her hired soldiers, and did not interfere with the Romans for a long time, while they went on to arrange the government of Sicily into what they called a province, which was ruled by a proprætor for a year after his magistracy at home. The Greek kingdom of Syracuse indeed still remained as an ally of Rome, and Messina and a few other cities were allowed to choose their own magistrates and govern themselves.

Soon after, Sardinia and Corsica were given up to the Romans by the hired armies of the Carthaginians, and as the natives fought hard against Rome, when they were conquered they were for the most part sold as slaves. These two islands likewise had a proprætor.

The Romans now had all the peninsula south of themselves, and as far north as Ariminim (now shortened into Rimini), but all beyond belonged to the Gauls — the Cisalpine Gauls, or Gauls on this side the Alps, as the Romans called them; while those on the other side were called Transalpine Gauls, or Gauls across the Alps. These northern Gauls were gathering again for an inroad on the south, and in the midst of the rumors of this danger there was a great thunderstorm at Rome, and the Capitol was struck by lightning. The Sybilline books were searched into to see what this might mean, and a warning was found, "Beware of the Gauls." Moreover, there was a saying that the Greeks and Gauls should one day enjoy the Forum; but the Romans fancied they could satisfy this prophecy by burying a man and woman of each nation, slaves, in the middle of the Forum, and then they prepared to attack the Gauls in their own country before the inroad could be made. There was a great deal of hard fighting, lasting for years; and in the course of it the consul, Caius Flaminius, began the great road which has since been called after him the Flaminian Way, and was the great northern road from Rome, as the Appian Way was the southern.

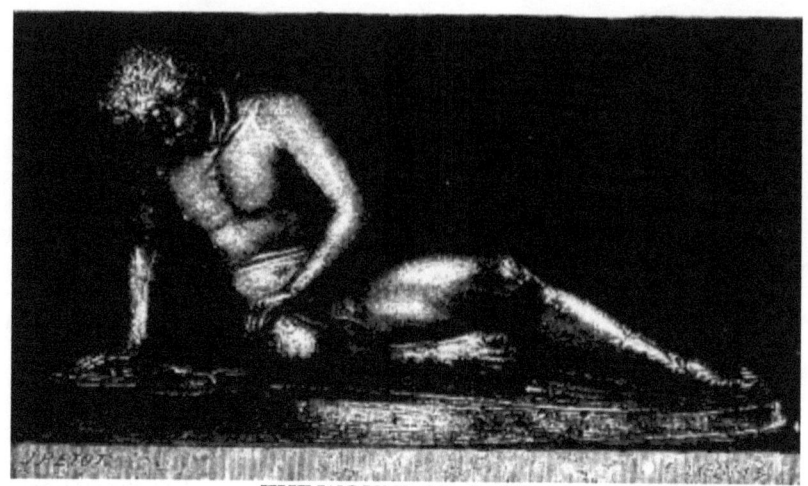

THE WOUNDED GAUL.

The great hero of the war was Marcus Claudius Marcellus, who had already made himself known for his dauntless courage. As consul, he fought a desperate battle on the banks of the Po with the Gauls of both sides the Alps, and himself killed their king or chief, Viridomar. He brought the spoils to Rome, and hung them in the Temple of Jupiter. It was only the third time in the history of Rome that such a thing had been done. Cisalpine Gaul was thus subdued, and another road was made to secure it; while in the short peace that followed the gates of the Temple of Janus were shut, having stood open ever since the reign of Numa.

The Romans were beginning to make their worship the same with that of the Greeks. They sent offerings to Greek temples, said that their old gods were the same as those of the Greeks, only under different names, and sent an embassy to Epidaurus to ask for a statue of Esculapius, the god of medicine and son of Phoebus Apollo. The emblem of Esculapius was a serpent, and tame serpents were kept about his temple at Epidaurus. One of these glided into the Roman galley that had come for the statue, and it was treated with great respect by all the crew until they sailed up the Tiber, when it made its way out of the vessel and swam to the island which had been formed by the settling of the mud round the heap of corn that had been thrown into the river when Porsena wasted the country. This was supposed to mean that the god himself took possession of the place, and a splendid temple there rose in his honor.

Another imitation of the Greeks which came into fashion at this time had a sad effect on the Romans. The old funerals in Greek poems had ended by games and struggles between swordsmen. Two brothers of the Brutus family first showed off such a game at their father's funeral, and it became a regular custom, not only at funerals, but whenever there was need to entertain the people, to show off fights of swordsmen. The soldier captives from conquered nations were used in this way; and some persons kept schools of slaves, who were trained for these fights and called gladiators. The battle was a real one, with sharp weapons, for life or death; and when a man was struck down, he was allowed to live or sentenced to death according as the spectators turned down or turned up their thumbs. The Romans fancied that the sight trained them to be brave, and to despise death and wounds; but the truth was that it only made them hard-hearted, and taught them to despise other people's pain — a very different thing from despising their own.

Another thing that did great harm was the making it lawful for a man to put away a wife who had no children. This ended by making the Romans much less careful to have one good wife, and the Roman ladies became much less noble and excellent than they had been in the good old days.

In the meantime, the Carthaginians, having lost the three islands, began to spread their settlements further in Spain, where their chief colony was New Carthage, or, as we call it, Carthagena. The mountains were full of gold mines, and the Iberians, the nation who held them, were brave and warlike, so that there was much fighting to train up fresh armies.

HANNIBAL'S VOW.

Hamilcar, the chief general in command there, had four sons, whom he said were lion whelps being bred up against Rome. He took them with him to Spain, and at a great sacrifice for the success of his arms the youngest and most promising, Hannibal, a boy of nine years old, was made to lay his hand on the altar of Baal and take an oath that he would always be the enemy of the Romans. Hamilcar was killed in battle, but Hannibal grew up to be all that he had hoped, and at twenty-six was in command of the army. He threatened the Iberians of Saguntum, who sent to ask help from Rome. A message was sent to him to forbid him to disturb the ally of Rome; but he had made up his mind for war, and never even asked the Senate of Carthage what was to be done, but went on with the siege of Saguntum. Rome was busy with a war in Illyria, and could send no help, and the Saguntines held out with the greatest bravery and constancy, month after month, till they were all on the point of starvation, then kindled a great fire, slew all their wives and children, and let Hannibal win nothing but a pile of smoking ruins.

IN THE PYRENEES.

Again the Romans sent to Carthage to complain, but the Senate there had made up their minds that war there must be, and that it was a good time when Rome had a war in Illyria on her hands, and Cisalpine Gaul hardly subdued; and they had such a general as Hannibal, though they did not know what a wonderful scheme he had in his mind, namely, to make his way by land from Spain to Italy, gaining the help of the Gauls, and stirring up all those nations of Italy who had fought so long against Rome. His march, which marks the beginning of the Second Punic War, started from the banks of the Ebro in the beginning of the summer of 219. His army was 20,000 foot and 12,000 horse, partly Carthaginian, partly Gaul and Iberian. The horsemen were Moorish, and he had thirty-seven elephants. He left his brother Hasdrubal with 10,000 men at the foot of the Pyrenees and pushed on, but he could not reach the Alps before the late autumn, and his passage is one of the greatest wonders of history. Roads there were none, and he had to force his way up the passes of the Little St. Bernard through snow and ice, terrible to the men and animals of Africa, and fighting all the way, so that men and horses perished in great numbers, and only seven of the elephants were left when he at length descended into the plains of Northern Italy, where he hoped the Cisalpine Gauls would welcome him.

CHAPTER XIX.
THE SECOND PUNIC WAR.
219.

When the Romans heard that Hannibal had passed the Pyrenees, they had two armies on foot, one under Publius Cornelius Scipio, which was to go to Spain, and the other under Tiberius Sempronius Longus, to attack Africa. They changed their plan, and kept Sempronius to defend Italy, while Scipio went by sea to Marsala, a Greek colony in Gaul, to try to stop Hannibal at the Rhone; but he was too late, and therefore, sending on most of his army to Spain, he came back himself with his choicest troops. With these he tried to stop the enemy from crossing the river Ticinus, but he was defeated and so badly wounded that his life was only saved by the bravery of his son, who led him out of the battle.

MEETING OF HANNIBAL AND SCIPIO AT ZAMA.

Before he was able to join the army again, Sempronius had fought another battle with Hannibal on the banks of the Trebia and suffered a terrible defeat. But winter now came on, and the Carthaginians found it very hard to bear in the marshes of the Arno. Hannibal himself was so ill that he only owed his life to the last of his elephants, which carried him safely through when he was almost blind, and in the end he lost an eye. In the spring he went on ravaging the country in hopes to make the two new consuls, Flaminius and Servilius, fight with him, but they were too cautious, until at last Flaminius attacked him in a heavy fog on the shore of Lake Trasimenus. It is said that an earthquake shook the ground, and that the eager warriors never perceived it; but again the Romans lost, Flaminius was killed, and there was a dreadful slaughter, for Hannibal had sworn to give no quarter to a Roman. The only thing that was hopeful for Rome was that neither Gauls, Etruscans, nor Italians showed any desire to rise in favor of Hannibal; and though he was now very near Rome, he durst not besiege it without the help of the people around to bring him supplies, so he only marched southwards, hoping to gain the support of the Greek colonies. A dictator was appointed, Quintus Fabius Maximus, who saw that, by strengthening all the garrisons in the towns and cutting off all provisions, he should wear the enemy out at last. As he always put off a battle, he was called Cunctator, or the Delayer; but at last he had the Carthaginians enclosed as in a trap in the valley of the river Vulturnus, and hoped to cut them off, posting men in ambush to fall on them on their morning's march. Hannibal guessed that this must be the plan; and at night he had the cattle in the camp collected, fastened torches to their horns, and drove them up the hills. The Romans, fancying themselves surrounded by the enemy, came out of their hiding-places to fall back on the camp, and Hannibal and his army safely escaped. This mischance made the Romans weary of the Delayer's policy, and when the year was out, and two consuls came in, though one of them, Lucius Æmilius Paulus, would have gone on in the same cautious plan of starving Hannibal out without a battle, the other, Caius Terentius Varro, who commanded on alternate days with him, was determined on a battle. Hannibal so contrived that it was fought on the plain of Cannæ, where there was plenty of space to use his Moorish horse. It was Varro's day of command, and he dashed at the centre of the enemy; Hannibal opened a space for him, then closed in on both sides with his terrible horse, and made a regular slaughter of the Romans. The last time that the consul Æmilius was seen was by a tribune named Lentulus, who found him sitting on a stone faint and bleeding, and would have given him his own horse to escape, but Æmilius answered that he had no mind to have to accuse his comrade of rashness, and had rather die. A troop of enemies coming up, Lentulus rode off, and looking back, saw his consul fall, pierced with darts. So many Romans had been killed, that Hannibal sent to Carthage a basket containing 10,000 of the gold rings worn by the knights.

ARCHIMEDES.

Hannibal was only five days' march beyond Rome, and his officers wanted him to turn back and attack it in the first shock of the defeat, but he could not expect to succeed without more aid from home, and he wanted to win over the Greek cities of the south; so he wintered in Campania, waiting for the fresh troops he expected from Africa or from Spain, where his brother Mago was preparing an army. But the Carthaginians did not care about Hannibal's campaigns in Italy, and sent no help; and Publius Cornelius Scipio and his brother, with a Roman army in Spain, were watching Mago and preventing him from marching, until at last he gave them battle and defeated and killed them both. But he was not allowed to go to Italy to his brother, who, in the meantime, found his army so unstrung and ill-disciplined in the delightful but languid Campania, that the Romans declared the luxuries of Capua were their best allies. He stayed in the south, however, trying to gain the alliance of the king of Macedon, and stirring up Syracuse to revolt. Marcellus, who was consul for the third time, was sent to reduce the city, which made a famous defence, for it contained Archimedes, the greatest mathematician of his time, who devised wonderful machines for crushing the besiegers in unexpected ways; but at last Marcellus found a weak part of the walls and surprised the citizens. He had given orders that Archimedes should be saved, but a soldier broke into the philosopher's room without knowing him, and found him so intent on his study that he had never heard the storming of the city. The man brandished his sword. "Only wait," muttered Archimedes, "till I have found out my problem;" but the man, not understanding him, killed him.

Hannibal remained in Italy, maintaining himself there with wonderful skill, though with none of the hopes with which he had set out. His brother Hasdrubal did succeed in leaving Spain with an army to help him, but was met on the river Metaurus by Tiberius Claudius Nero, beaten, and slain. His head was cut off by Nero's order, and thrown into Hannibal's camp to give tidings of his fate.

Young Scipio, meantime, had been sent to Spain, where he gained great advantages, winning the friendship of the Iberians, and gaining town after town till Mago had little left but Gades and the extreme south. Scipio was one of the noblest of the Romans, brave, pious, and what was more unusual, of such sweet and winning temper, that it was said of him that wherever he went he might have been a king.

On returning to Rome, he showed the Senate that the best way to get Hannibal out of Italy was to attack Africa. Cautious old Fabius doubted, but Scipio was sent to Sicily, where he made an alliance with Massinissa, the Moorish king in Africa; and, obtaining leave to carry out his plan, he was sent thither, and so alarmed Carthage, that Hannibal was recalled to defend his own country, where he had not been since he was a child. A great battle took place at Zama between him and Hannibal, in which Scipio was the conqueror, and the loss of Carthage was so terrible that the Romans were ready to have marched in on her and made her their subject, but Scipio persuaded them to be forbearing. Carthage was to pay an immense tribute, and swear never to make war on any ally of Rome. And thus ended the Second Punic War, in the year 201.

CHAPTER XX.
THE FIRST EASTERN WAR.
215-183.

Scipio remained in Africa till he had arranged matters and won such a claim to Massinissa's gratitude that this king of Numidia was sure to watch over the interests of Rome. Scipio then returned home, and entered Rome with a grand triumph, all the nobler for himself that he did not lead Hannibal in his chains. He had been too generous to demand that so brave an enemy should be delivered up to him. He received the surname of Africanus, and was one of the most respected and beloved of Romans. He was the first who began to take up Greek learning and culture, and to exchange the old Roman ruggedness for the graces of philosophy and poetry. Indeed the Romans were beginning to have much to do with the Greeks, and the war they entered upon now was the first for the sake of spreading their own power. All the former ones had been in self-defence, and the new one did in fact spring out of the Punic war, for the Carthaginians had tried to persuade Philip, king of Macedon, to follow in the track of Pyrrhus, and come and help Hannibal in Southern Italy. The Romans had kept him off by stirring up the robber Ætolians against him; and when he began to punish these wild neighbors, the Romans leagued themselves with the old Greek cities which Macedon oppressed, and a great war took place.

Titus Quinctius Flaminius commanded in Greece for four years, first as consul and then as proconsul. His crowning victory was at Cynocephalæ, or the Dogshead Rocks, where he so broke the strength of Macedon that at the Isthmian games he proclaimed the deliverance of Greece, and in their joy the people crowded round him with crowns and garlands, and shouted so loud that birds in the air were said to have dropped down at the sound.

Macedon had cities in Asia Minor, and the king of Syria's enemy, Antiochus the Great, hoped to master them, and even to conquer Greece by the help of Hannibal, who had found himself unable to live in Carthage after his defeat, and was wandering about to give his services to any one who was a foe of Rome.

As Rome took the part of Philip, as her subject and ally, there was soon full scope for his efforts; but the Syrians were such wretched troops that even Hannibal could do nothing with them, and the king himself would not attend to his advice, but wasted his time in pleasure in the isle of Euboea. So the consul Acilius first beat them at Thermopylæ, and then, on Lucius Cornelius Scipio being sent to conduct the war, his great brother Africanus volunteered to go with him as his lieutenant, and together they followed Antiochus into Asia Minor, and gained such advantages that the Syrian was obliged to sue for peace. The Romans replied by requiring of him to give up all Asia Minor as far as Mount Tarsus, and in despair he risked a battle in Magnesia, and met with a total defeat; 80,000 Greeks and Syrians being overthrown by 50,000 Romans. Neither Africanus nor Hannibal were present in this battle, since the first was ill, and the second was besieged in a city in Pamphylia; but while terms of peace were being made, the two are said have met on friendly terms, and Scipio asked Hannibal whom he thought the greatest of generals. "Alexander," was the answer. "Whom the next greatest?" "Pyrrhus." "Whom do you rank as the third?" "Myself," said Hannibal. "But if you had beaten me?" asked Scipio. "Then I would have placed myself before Alexander."

HANNIBAL

The Romans insisted that Hannibal should be dismissed by Antiochus, though Scipio declared that this was ungenerous; but they dreaded his never-ceasing enmity; and when he took refuge with the king of Bothnia, they still required that he should be given up or driven a way. On this, Hannibal, worn-out and disappointed, put an end to his own life by poison, saying he would rid the Romans of their fear of an old man.

The provinces taken from Antiochus were given to Eumenes, king of Pergamus, who was to reign over them as tributary to the Romans. Lucius Scipio received the surname of Asiaticus, and the two brothers returned to Rome; but they had been too generous and merciful to the conquered to suit the grasping spirit that had begun to prevail at Rome, and directly after his triumph Lucius was accused of having taken to himself an undue share of the spoil. His brother was too indignant at the shameful accusation to think of letting him justify himself, but tore up his accounts in the face of the people. The tribune, Nævius, thereupon spitefully called upon him to give an account of the spoil of Carthage taken twenty years before. The only reply he gave was to exclaim, "This is the day of the victory of Zama. Let us give thanks to the gods for it;" and he led all that was noble and good in Rome with him to the temple of Jupiter and offered the anniversary sacrifice. No one durst say another word against him or his brother; but he did not choose to remain among the citizens who had thus insulted him, but went away to his estate at Liternum, and when he died, desired to be buried there, saying that he would not even leave his bones to his ungrateful country. The Cornelian family was the only one among the higher Romans who buried instead of burning their dead. He left no son, only a daughter, who was married to Tiberius Sempronius Gracchus, a brave officer who was among those who were sent to finish reducing Spain. It was a long, terrible war, fought city by city, inch by inch; but Gracchus is said to have taken no less than three hundred fortresses. But he was a milder conqueror than some of the Romans, and tried to tame and civilize the wild races instead of treating them with the terrible severity shown by Marcus Porcius Cato, the sternest of all old Romans. However, by the year 178 Spain had been reduced to obedience, and the cities and the coast were in good order, though the mountains harbored fierce tribes always ready for revolt.

Gracchus died early, and Cornelia, his widow, devoted herself to the cause of his three children, refusing to be married again, which was very uncommon in a Roman lady. When a lady asked her to show her her ornaments, she called her two boys, Tiberius and Caius, and their sister Sempronia, and said, "These are my jewels;" and when she was complimented on being the daughter of Africanus, she said that the honor she should care more for was the being called "the mother of the Gracchi."

It was not, however, one of her sons that was chosen to carry on their grandfather's name and the sacrifices of the Cornelian family. Probably Caius was not born when Scipio died, for his choice had been the second son of his sister and of Lucius Æmilius Paulus (son of him who died at Cannæ.) This child being adopted by his uncle, was called Publius Cornelius Scipio Æmilianus, and when he grew up was to marry his cousin Sempronia.

CHAPTER XXI.
THE CONQUEST OF GREECE, CORINTH, AND CARTHAGE.
179 — 145.

It was a great change when Rome, which to the Greeks of Pyrrhus' time had seemed so rude and simple, was thought such a school of policy that Greek and half-Greek kings sent their sons to be educated there, partly as hostages for their own peaceableness, and partly to learn the spirit of Roman rule. The first king who did this was Philip of Macedon, who sent his son Demetrius to be brought up at Rome; but when he came back, his father and brother were jealous of him, and he was soon put to death.

When his brother Perseus came to the throne, there was hatred between him and the Romans, and ere long he was accused of making war on their allies. He offered to make peace, but they replied that they would hear nothing till he had laid down his arms, and this he would not do, so that Lucius Æmilius Paulus (the brother-in-law of Scipio) was sent to reduce him. As Æmilius came into his own house after receiving the appointment, he met his little daughter crying, and when he asked her what was the matter, she answered, "Oh, father, Perseus is dead!" She meant her little dog, but he kissed her and thanked her for the good omen. He overran Macedon, and gained the great battle of Pydna, after which Perseus was obliged to give himself up into the hands of the Romans, begging, however, not to be made to walk in Æmilius' triumph. The general answered that he might obtain that favor from himself, meaning that he could die by his own hand; but Perseus did not take the hint, which seems to us far more shocking than it did to a Roman; he did walk in the triumph, and died a few years after in Italy. Æmilius' two sons were with him throughout this campaign, though still boys under Polybius, their Achaian tutor. Macedon was divided into four provinces, and became entirely subject to Rome.

CORINTH.

The Greeks of the Achaian League began to have quarrels among themselves, and when the Romans interfered a fierce spirit broke out, and they wanted to have their old freedom, forgetting how entirely unable they were to stand against the power of the Romans. Caius Cæcilius Metellus, a man of one of the best and most gracious Roman families, was patient with them and did his best to pacify them, being most unwilling to ruin the noble old historical cities; but these foolish Greeks fancied that his kindness showed weakness, and forced on the war, sending a troop to guard the pass of Thermopylæ, but they were swept away. Unfortunately, Metellus had to go out of office, and Lucius Mummius, a fierce, rude, and ignorant soldier, came in his stead to complete the conquest. Corinth was taken, utterly ruined and plundered throughout, and a huge amount of treasure was sent to Rome, as well as pictures and statues famed all over the world. Mummius was very much laughed at for having been told they must be carried in his triumph; and yet, not understanding their beauty, he told the sailors to whose charge they were given, that if they were lost, new ones must be supplied. However, he was an honest man, who did not help himself out of the plunder, as far too many were doing. After that, Achaia was made a Roman province.

At this time the third and last Punic war was going on. The old Moorish king, Massinissa, had been continually tormenting Carthage ever since she had been weak, and declaring that Phoenician strangers had no business in Africa. The Carthaginians, who had no means of defending themselves, complained; but the Romans would not listen, hoping, perhaps, that they would be goaded at last into attacking the Moor, and thus giving a pretext for a war. Old Marcus Porcius Cato, who was sent on a message to Carthage, came back declaring that it was not safe to let so mighty a city of enemies stand so near. He brought back a branch of figs fresh and good, which he showed the Senate in proof of how near she was, and ended each sentence with saying, "*Delenda est Carthago*" (Carthage is to be wiped out). He died that same year at ninety years old, having spent most of his life in making a staunch resistance to the easy and luxurious fashions that were coming in with wealth and refinement. One of his sayings always deserves to be remembered. When he was opposing a law giving permission to the ladies to wear gold and purple, he said they would all be vying with one another, and that the poor would be ashamed of not making as good an appearance as the rich. "And," said he, "she who blushes for doing what she ought, will soon cease to blush for doing what she ought not."

One wonders he did not see that to have no enemy near at hand to guard against was the very worst thing for the hardy, plain old ways he was so anxious to keep up. However, Carthage was to be wiped out, and Scipio Æmilianus was sent to do the terrible work. He defeated Hasdrubal, the last of the Carthaginian generals, and took the citadel of Byrsa; but though all hope was over, the city held out in utter desperation. Weapons were forged out of household implements, even out of gold and silver, and the women twisted their long hair into bow-strings; and when the walls were stormed, they fought from street to street and house to house, so that the Romans gained little but ruins and dead bodies. Carthage and Corinth fell on the same day of the year 179.

Part of Spain still had to be subdued, and Scipio Æmilianus was sent thither. The city of Numantia, with only 5000 inhabitants, endured one of those long, hopeless sieges for which Spanish cities have in all times been remarkable, and was only taken at last when almost every citizen had perished.

At the same time, Attalus, king of Pergamus in Asia Minor, being the last of his race, bequeathed his dominions to the Romans, and thus gave them their first solid footing there.

All this was altering Roman manners much. Weak as the Greeks were, their old doings of every kind were still the admiration of every one, and the Romans, who had always been rough, straightforward doers, began to wish to learn of them to think. All the wealthier families had Greeks for tutors for their sons, and expected them to talk and write the language, and study the philosophy and poetry till they should be as familiar with it as if they were Greeks themselves. Unluckily, the Greeks themselves had fallen from their earnestness and greatness, so that there was not much to be learnt of them now but vain deceit and bad taste.

Rich Romans, too, began to get most absurdly luxurious. They had splendid villas on the Italian hill-sides, where they went to spend the summer when Rome was unhealthy, and where they had beautiful gardens, with courts paved with mosaic, and fish-ponds for the pet fish for which many had a passion. One man was laughed at for having shed tears when his favorite fish died, and he retorted by saying that it was more than his accuser had done for his wife.

Their feasts were as luxurious as they could make them, in spite of laws to keep them within bounds. Dishes of nightingales' tongues, of fatted dormice, and even of snails, were among their food: and sometimes a stream was made to flow along the table, containing the living companion of the mullet which served as part of the meal.

CHAPTER XXII.
THE GRACCHI.
137-122.

Young Tiberius Sempronius Gracchus, the eldest of Cornelia's jewels, was sent in the year 137 to join the Roman army in Spain. As he went through Etruria, which, as every one knew, had been a thickly peopled, fertile country in old times, he was shocked to see its dreariness and desolation. Instead of farms and vineyards, there were great bare spaces of land, where sheep, kids, or goats were feeding. These vast tracts belonged to Romans, who kept slaves to attend to the flocks; while all the corn that was used in Rome came from Sicily or Africa, and the poorer Romans lived in the city itself — idle men, chiefly trusting to distributions of corn, and unable to work for themselves because they had no ground to till; and as to trades and handicrafts, the rich men had everything they wanted made in their own houses by their slaves.

CORNELIA AND HER SONS.

No wonder the Romans were losing their old character. This was the very thing that the Licinian law had been intended to prevent, by forbidding any citizen to have more than a certain quantity of land, and giving the state the power of resuming it. The law was still there, but it had been disused and forgotten; estates had been gathered into the hands of families and handed down, till now, though there were 400,000 citizens, only 2,000 were men of property.

While Tiberius was serving in Spain, he decided on his plan. As his family was plebeian, he could be a tribune of the people, and as soon as he came home he stood and was elected. Then he proposed reviving the Licinian law, that nobody should have more than 500 acres, and that the rest should be divided among those who had nothing, leaving, however, a larger portion to those who had many children.

There was, of course, a terrible uproar; the populace clamoring for their rights, and the rich trying to stop the measure. They bribed one of the other tribunes to forbid it; but there was a fight, in which Tiberius prevailed, and he and his young brother Caius, and his father-in-law Appius Claudius, were appointed as triumvers to see the law carried out. Then the rich men followed their old plan of spreading reports among the people that Tiberius wanted to make himself a king, and had accepted a crown and purple robe from some foreign envoy. When his year of office was coming to an end, he sought to be elected tribune again, but the patricians said it was against the law. There was a great tumult, in the course of which he put his hand to his head, either to guard it from a blow or to beckon his friends. "He demands the diadem," shouted his enemies, and there was a great struggle, in which three hundred people were killed. Tiberius tried to take refuge in the Temple of Jupiter, but the doors were closed against him; he stumbled, was knocked down with a club, and killed.

However, the Sempronian law had been made, and the people wanted, of course, to have it carried out, while the nobles wanted it to be a dead letter. Scipio Æmilianus, the brother-in-law of the Gracchi, had been in Spain all this time, but he had so much disapproved of Tiberius' doings that he was said to have exclaimed, on hearing of his death, "So perish all who do the like." But when he came home, he did so much to calm and quiet matters, that there was a cry to make him Dictator, and let him settle the whole matter. Young Caius Gracchus, who thought the cause would thus be lost, tried to prevent the choice by fixing on him the name of tyrant. To which Scipio calmly replied, "Rome's enemies may well wish me dead, for they know that while I live Rome cannot perish."

When he went home, he shut himself into his room to prepare his discourse for the next day, but in the morning he was found dead, without a wound, though his slaves declared he had been murdered. Some suspected his wife Sempronia, others even her mother Cornelia, but the Senate would not have the matter enquired into. He left no child, and the Africanus line of Cornelius ended with him.

Caius Gracchus was nine years younger than his brother, and was elected tribune as soon as he was old enough. He was full of still greater schemes than his brother. His mother besought him to be warned by his brother's fate, but he was bent on his objects, and carried some of them out. He had the Sempronian law reaffirmed, though he could not act on it; but in the meantime he began a regular custom of having corn served out to the poorer citizens, and found work for them upon roads and bridges; also he caused the state to clothe the soldiers, instead of their doing it at their own expense. Another scheme which he first proposed was to make the Italians of the countries now one with Roman territory into citizens, with votes like the Romans themselves; but this again angered the patricians, who saw they should be swamped by numbers and lose their power.

He also wanted to found a colony of plebeians on the ruins of Carthage, and when his tribuneship was over he went to Africa to see about it; but when he came home the patricians had arranged an attack on him, and he was insulted by the lictor of the consul Opimius. The patricians collected on one side, the poorer sort around Caius on the Aventine Hill; but the nobles were the strongest, the plebeians fled, and Caius withdrew with one slave into a sacred grove, whence he hoped to reach the Tiber; but the wood was surrounded, his retreat was cut off, and he commanded the slave to kill him that he might not fall alive into the hands of his enemies, after which the poor faithful fellow killed himself, unable to bear the loss of his master. The weight of Caius' head in gold had been promised by the Senate, and the man who found the body was said to have taken out the brains and filled it up with lead that his reward might be larger. Three thousand men were killed in this riot, ten times as many as at Tiberius' death.

Opimius was so proud of having overthrown Caius, that he had a medal struck with Hercules slaying the monsters. Cornelia, broken-hearted, retired to a country-house; but in a few years the feeling turned, great love was shown to the memory of the two brothers, statues were set up in their honor, and when Cornelia herself died, her statue was inscribed with the title she had coveted, "The mother of the Gracchi."

ROMAN CENTURION.

Things were indeed growing worse and worse. The Romans were as brave as ever in the field, and were sure in the end to conquer any nation they came in contact with; but at home, the city was full of overgrown rich men, with huge hosts of slaves, and of turbulent poor men, who only cared for their citizenship for the sake of the corn they gained by it, and the games exhibited by those who stood for a magistracy. Immense sums were spent in hiring gladiators and bringing wild animals to be baited for their amusement; and afterwards, when sent out to govern the provinces, the expenses were repaid by cruel grinding and robbing the people of the conquered states.

CHAPTER XXIII.
THE WARS OF MARIUS.
106-98.

After the death of Massinissa, king of Numidia, the ally of the Romans, there were disputes among his grandsons, and Jugurtha, whom they held to have the least right, obtained the kingdom. The commander of the army sent against him was Caius Marius, who had risen from being a free Roman peasant in the village of Arpinum, but serving under Scipio Æmilianus, had shown such ability, that when some one was wondering where they would find the equal of Scipio when he was gone, that general touched the shoulder of his young officer and said, "Possibly here."

Rough soldier as he always was, he married Julia, of the high family of the Cæsars, who were said to be descended from Æneas; and though he was much disliked by the Senate, he always carried the people with him. When he received the province of Numidia, instead of, as every one had done before, forming his army only of Roman citizens, he offered to enlist whoever would, and thus filled his ranks with all sorts of wild and desperate men, whom he could indeed train to fight, but who had none of the old feeling for honor or the state, and this in the end made a great change in Rome.

Jugurtha maintained a wild war in the deserts of Africa with Marius, but at last he was betrayed to the Romans by his friend Bocchus, another Moorish king, and Lucius Cornelius Sulla, Marius' lieutenant, was sent to receive him — a transaction which Sulla commemorated on a signet ring which he always wore. Poor Jugurtha was kept two years to appear at the triumph, where he walked in chains, and then was thrown alive into the dungeon under the Capitol, where he took six days to die of cold and hunger.

Marius was elected consul for the second time even before he had quite come home from Africa, for it was a time of great danger. Two fierce and terrible tribes, whom the Romans called

Cimbri and Teutones, and who were but the vanguard of the swarms who would overwhelm them six centuries later, had come down through Germany to the settled countries belonging to Rome, especially the lands round the old Greek settlements in Gaul, which had fallen of course into the hands of the Romans, and were full of beautiful rich cities, with houses and gardens round them. The Province, as the Romans called it, would have been grand plundering ground for these savages, and Marius established himself in a camp on the banks of the Rhone to protect it, cutting a canal to bring his provisions from the sea, which still remains. While he was thus engaged, he was a fourth time elected consul.

MARIUS.

The enemy began to move. The Cimbri meant to march eastward round the Alps, and pour through the Tyrol into Italy; the Teutones to go by the West, fighting Marius on the way. But he would not come out of his camp on the Rhone, though the Teutones, as they passed, shouted to ask the Roman soldiers what messages they had to send to their wives in Italy.

When they had all passed, he came out of his camp and followed them as far as Aquæ Sextiæ, now called Aix, where one of the most terrible battles the world ever saw was fought. These people were a whole tribe — wives, children, and everything they had with them — and to be defeated was utter and absolute ruin. A great enclosure was made with their carts and wagons, whence the women threw arrows and darts to help the men; and when, after three days of hard fighting, all hope was over, they set fire to the enclosure and killed their children and themselves. The whole swarm was destroyed. Marius marched away, and no one was left to bury the dead, so that the spot was called the Putrid Fields, and is still known as Les Pourrieres.

While Marius was offering up the spoil, tidings came that he was a fifth time chosen consul; but he had to hasten into Italy, for the other consul, Catulus, could not stand before the Cimbri, and Marius met him on the Po retreating from them. The Cimbri demanded lands in Italy for themselves and their allies the Teutones. "The Teutones have all the ground they will ever want, on the other side the Alps," said Marius; and a terrible battle followed, in which the Cimbri were as entirely cut off as their allies had been.

Marius was made consul a sixth time. As a reward to the brave soldiers who had fought under him, he made one thousand of them, who came from the city of Camerinum, Roman citizens, and this the patricians disliked greatly. His excuse was, "The din of arms drowned the voice of the law;" but the new citizens were provided for by lands in the Province, which the Romans said the Gauls had lost to the Teutones and they had reconquered. It was very hard on the Gauls, but that was the last thing a Roman cared about.

ONE OF THE TROPHIES, CALLED OF MARIUS, AT THE CAPITOL AT ROME.

The Italians, however, were all crying out for the rights of Romans, and the more far-sighted among the Romans would, like Caius Gracchus, have granted them. Marcus Livius Drusus did his best for them; he was a good man, wise and frank-hearted. When he was having a house built, and the plan was shown him which would make it impossible for any one to see into it, he said, "Rather build one where my fellow-countrymen may see all I do." He was very much loved, and when he was ill, prayers were offered at the temples for his recovery; but no sooner did he take up the cause of the Italians than all the patricians hated him bitterly. "Rome for the Romans," was their watchword. Drusus was one day entertaining an Italian gentleman, when his little nephew, Marcus Porcius Cato, a descendant of the old censor, and bred in stern patrician views, was playing about the room. The Italian merrily asked him to favor his cause. "No," said the boy. He was offered toys and cakes if he would change his mind, but he still refused; he was threatened, and at last he was held by one leg out of the window — all without shaking his resolution for a moment; and this constancy he carried with him through life.

People's minds grew embittered, and Drusus was murdered in the street, crying as he fell, "When will Rome find so good a citizen!" After this, the Italians took up arms, and what was called the Social War began. Marius had no high command, being probably too much connected with the enemy. Some of the Italian tribes held with Rome, and these were rewarded with the citizenship; and after all, though the consul Lucius Julius Cæsar, brother-in-law to Marius, gained some victories, the revolt was so widespread, that the Senate felt it wisest, on the first sign of peace, to offer citizenship to such Italians as would come within sixty days to claim it. Citizenship brought a man under Roman law, freed him from taxation, and gave him many advantages and openings to a rise in life. But he could only give his vote at Rome, and only there receive the distribution of corn, and he further became liable to be called out to serve in a legion, so that the benefit was not so great as at first appeared, and no very large numbers of Italians came to apply for it.

CHAPTER XXIV.
THE ADVENTURES OF MARIUS.
93 — 84.

The chief foe of Marius was almost always his second in command, Publius Cornelius Sulla, one of the men of highest family in Rome. He had all the high culture and elegant learning that the rough soldier Marius despised, spoke and wrote Greek as easily as Latin, and was as well read in Greek poetry and philosophy as any Athenian could be; but he was given up to all the excesses of luxury in which the wealthy Romans indulged, and his way of life had made him frightful to look at. His face was said to be like a mulberry sprinkled with salt, with a terrible pair of blue eyes glaring out of it.

In 93 he was sent to command against Mithridates, king of Pontus, one of the little kingdoms in Asia Minor that had sprung up out of the break-up of Alexander's empire. Under this king, Mithridates, it had grown very powerful. He was of Persian birth, had all the learning and science both of Greece and the far East, and was said in especial to be wonderfully learned in all plants and their virtues, so as to have made himself proof against all kinds of poison, and he could speak twenty-five languages.

He had great power in Asia Minor, and took upon himself to appoint a king of Cappadocia, thus leading to a quarrel with the Romans. In the midst of the Social War, when he thought they had their hands full in Italy, Mithridates caused all the native inhabitants of Asia Minor to rise upon the Romans among them in one night and murder them all, so that 80,000 are said to have perished. Sulla was ordered to take the command of the army which was to avenge their death; but, while he was raising his forces, Marius, angry that the patricians had hindered the plebeians and Italians from gaining more by the Social War, raised up a great tumult, meaning to overpower the patricians' resistance. He would have done more wisely had he waited until Sulla was quite gone, for that general came back to the rescue of his friends with six newly-raised legions, and Marius could only just contrive to escape from Rome, where he was proclaimed a traitor and a price set on his head. He was now seventy years old, but full of spirit. First he escaped to his own farm, whence he hoped to reach Ostia, where a ship was waiting for him; but a party of horsemen were seen coming, and he was hidden in a cart full of beans and driven down the coast, where he embarked, meaning to go to Africa; but adverse winds and want of food forced him to land at Circæum, whence, with a few friends, he made his way along the coast, through woods and rocks, keeping up the spirits of his companions by telling them that, when a little boy, he robbed an eyrie of seven eaglets, and that a soothsayer had then foretold that he would be seven times consul. At last a troop of horse was seen coming towards them, and at the same time two ships near the coast. The only hope was in swimming out to the nearest ship, and Marius was so heavy and old that this was done with great difficulty. Even then the ships were so near the shore that the pursuers could command the crew to throw Marius out, but this they refused to do, though they only waited till the soldiers were gone, to put him on shore again. Here he was in a marshy, boggy place, where an old man let him rest in his cottage, and then hid him in a cave under a heap of rushes. Again, however, the troops appeared, and threatened the old man for hiding an enemy of the Romans. It was in Marius' hearing, and fearing to be betrayed, he rushed out into a pool, where he stood up to his neck in water till a soldier saw him, and he was dragged out and taken to the city of Minturnæ.

There the council decided on his death, and sent a soldier to kill him, but the fierce old man stood glaring at him, and said. "Darest thou kill Caius Marius?" The man was so frightened that he ran away, crying out, "I cannot kill Caius Marius."

The Senate of Minturnæ took this as an omen, and remembered besides that he had been a good friend to the Italians, so they conducted him through a sacred grove to the sea, and sent him off to Africa.

THE CATAPULT.

On landing, he sent his son to ask shelter from one of the Numidian princes, and, while waiting for an answer, he was harassed by a messenger from a Roman officer of low rank, forbidding his presence in Africa. He made no reply till the messenger pressed to know what to say to his master. Then the old man looked up, and sternly answered. "Say that you have seen Caius Marius sitting in the ruins of Carthage" — a grand rebuke for the insult to fallen greatness. But the Numidian could not receive him, and he could only find shelter in a little island on the coast.

There he soon heard that no sooner had Sulla embarked for the East than Rome had fallen into dire confusion. The consuls, Caius Octavius and Publius Cornelius Cinna, were of opposite parties, and had a furious fight, in which Cinna was driven out of Rome, and at the same time the Italians had begun a new Social War. Marius saw that his time was come. He hurried to Etruria, where he was joined by a party of his friends and five hundred runaway slaves. The discontented Romans formed another army under Quintus Sertorius, and the Samnites, who had begun the war, overpowered the troops sent against them, and marched to Rome, declaring they would have no peace till they had destroyed the wolf's lair. Cinna and an army were advancing on another side, and, as he was really consul, the Senate in their distress admitted him, hoping that he would stop the rest; but when he marched in and seated himself again in the chair of office, he had by his side old Marius clothed in rags.

ISLAND ON THE COAST.

They were bent on revenge, and terrible it was, beginning with the consul, Caius Octavius, who had disdained to flee, and whose head was severed from his body and displayed in the Forum, with many other senators of the noblest blood in Rome, who had offended either Marius or Cinna or any of their fierce followers. Marius walked along in gloomy silence, answering no one; but his followers were bidden to spare only those to whom he gave his hand to be kissed. The slaves pillaged the houses, murdered many on their own account, and everything was in the wildest uproar, till the two chiefs called in Sertorius with a legion to restore order.

Then they named themselves consuls, without even asking for an election, and thus Marius was seven times consul. He wanted to go out to the East and take the command from Sulla, but his health was too much broken, and before the year of his consulate was over he died. The last time he had left the house, he had said to some friends that no man ought to trust again to such a doubtful fortune as his had been; and then he took to his bed for seven days without any known illness, and there was found dead, so that he was thought to have starved himself to death.

Cinna put in another consul named Valerius Flaccus, and invited all the Italians to enroll themselves as Roman citizens. Then Flaccus went out to the East, meaning to take away the command from Sulla, who was hunting Mithridates out of Greece, which he had seized and held for a short time. But Flaccus' own army rose against him and killed him, and Sulla, after beating Mithridates, driving him back to Pontus, and making peace with him, was now to come home.

CHAPTER XXV.
SULLA'S PROSCRIPTION.
88-71.

There was great fear at Rome, among the friends of Cinna and Marius, at the prospect of Sulla's return. A fire broke out in the Capitol, and this added to their terror, for the Books of the Sybil were burnt, and all her prophecies were lost. Cinna tried to oppose Sulla's landing, but was killed by his own soldiers at Brundusium.

Sulla, with his victorious army, could not be stopped. Sertorius fled to Spain, but Marius' son tried, with the help of the Samnites, to resist, and held out Præneste, but the Samnites were beaten in a terrible battle outside the walls, and when the people of the city saw the heads of the leaders carried on spear points, they insisted on giving up. Young Marius and a Samnite noble hid themselves in a cave, and as they had no hope, resolved to die; so they fought, hoping to kill each other, and when Marius was left alive, he caused himself to be slain by a slave.

Sulla marched on towards Rome, furious at the resistance he met with, and determined on a terrible vengeance. He could not enter the city till he was ready to dismiss his army and have his triumph, so the Senate came out to meet him in the temple of Bellona. As they took their seats, they heard dreadful shrieks and cries. "No matter," said Sulla; "it is only some wretches being punished." The wretches were the 8000 Samnite prisoners he had taken at the battle of Præneste, and brought to be killed in the Campus Martius; and with these shocking sounds to mark that he was in earnest, the purple-faced general told the trembling Senate that if they submitted to him he would be good to them, but that he would spare none of his enemies, great or small.

And his men were already in the city and country, slaughtering not only the party of Marius, but every one against whom any one of them had a spite, or whose property he coveted. Marius' body, which had been buried and not burnt, was taken from the grave and thrown into the Tiber; and such horrible deeds were done that Sulla was asked in the Senate where the execution was to stop. He showed a list of eighty more who had yet to die; and the next day and the next he brought other lists of two hundred and thirty each. These dreadful lists were called proscriptions, and any one who tried to shelter the victims was treated in the same manner. The property of all who were slain was seized, and their children declared incapable of holding any public office.

Among those who were in danger was the nephew of Marius' wife, Caius Julius Cæsar, but, as he was of a high patrician family, Sulla only required of him to divorce his wife and marry a stepdaughter of his own. Cæsar refused, and fled to the Sabine hills, where pursuers were sent after him; but his life was begged for by his friends at Rome, especially by the Vestal Virgins, and Sulla spared his life, saying, however, "Beware; in that young trifler is more than one Marius." Cæsar went to join the army in the East for safety, and thus broke off the idle life of pleasure he had been leading in Rome.

PALAZZO VECCHIO, FLORENCE.

The country people were even more cruelly punished than the citizens: whole cities were destroyed and districts laid waste; the whole of Etruria was ravaged, the old race entirely swept away, and the towns ruined beyond revival, while the new city of Florence was built with their remains, and all we know of them is from the tombs which have of late years been opened.

CORNELIUS SULLA.

Both the consuls had perished, and Sulla caused himself to be named Dictator. He had really a purpose in all the horrors he had perpetrated, namely, to clear the way for restoring the old government at Rome, which Marius and his Italians had been overthrowing. He did not see that the rule which had worked tolerably well while Rome was only a little city with a small country round it, would not serve when it was the head of numerous distant countries, where the governors, like himself and Marius, grew rich, and trained armies under them able to overpower the whole state at home. So he set to work to put matters as much as possible in the old order. So many of the Senate had been killed, that he had to make up the numbers by putting in three hundred knights; and, to supply the lack of other citizens, after the hosts who had perished, he allowed the Italians to go on coming in to be enrolled as citizens; and ten thousand slaves, who had belonged to his victims, were not only set free, but made citizens as his own clients, thus taking the name of Cornelius. He also much lessened the power of the tribunes of the people, and made a law that when a man had once been a tribune he should never be chosen for any of the higher offices of the state. By these means he sought to keep up the old patrician power, on which he believed the greatness of Rome depended; though, after all, the grand old patrician families had mostly died off, and half the Senate were only knights made noble.

After this Sulla resigned the dictatorship, for he was growing old, and had worn out his health by his riot and luxury. He spent his time in a villa near Rome, talking philosophy with his friends, and dictating the history of his own life in Greek. When he died, he bade them burn his body, contrary to the practice of the Cornelii, no doubt fearing it would be treated like that of Marius.

The most promising of the men of his party who were growing up and coming forward was Cnæus Pompeius, a brave and worthy man, who had while quite young, gained such a victory over a Numidian prince that Sulla himself gave him the title of Magnus, or the Great. He was afterwards sent to Spain, where Sertorius held out for eight years against the Roman power with the help of the native chiefs, but at last was put to death by his own followers. Things were altogether in a bad state. There were great struggles in Rome at every election, for the officers of the state were now chiefly esteemed for the sake of the three or five years' government in the provinces to which they led. No expense was thought too great in shows of beasts and gladiators by which to win the votes of the people; for, after the year of office, the candidate meant amply to repay himself by what he could squeeze out of the unhappy province under his charge, and nobody cared for cruelty or injustice to any one but a Roman citizen.

Numbers of gladiators were kept and trained to fight in these shows; and while the Spanish war was going on, a whole school of them — seventy-eight in number — who were kept at Capua, broke out, armed themselves with the spits, hooks, and axes in a butcher's shop, and took refuge in the crater of Mount Vesuvius, which at that time showed no signs of being an active volcano. There, under their leader Spartacus, they gathered together every gladiator slave or who could run away to them, and Spartacus wanted them to march northward, force their way through Italy, climb the Alps, and reach their homes in Thrace and Gaul; but the plunder of Italy tempted them, and they would not go, till an army was sent against them under Marcus Licinius Crassus — called Dives, or the Rich, from the spoil he had gained during the proscription. Then Spartacus hoped to escape in a fleet of pirate ships from Cilicia, and to hold out in the passes of Mount Taurus; but the Cilician pirates deceived him, sailed away with his money, and left him to his fate, and he and his gladiators were all slain by Crassus and Pompeius, who had been called home from Spain.

CHAPTER XXVI.
THE CAREER OF POMPEIUS.
70-63.

Cnæus Pompeius Magnus and Lucius Licinius Crassus Dives were consuls together in the year 70; but Crassus, though he feasted the people at 10,000 tables, was envied and disliked, and would never have been elected but for Pompeius, who was a great favorite with the people, and so much trusted, both by them and the nobles, that it seems to have filled him with pride, for he gave himself great airs, and did not treat his fellow-consul as an equal.

When his term of office was over, the most pressing thing to be done was to put down the Cilician pirates. In the angle formed between Asia Minor and Syria, with plenty of harbors formed by the spurs of Mount Taurus, there had dwelt for ages past a horde of sea robbers, whose swift galleys darted on the merchant ships of Tyre and Alexandria; and now, after the ruin of the Syrian kingdom, they had grown so rich that their state galleys had silken sails, oars inlaid with ivory and silver, and bronze prows. They robbed the old Greek temples and the Eastern shrines, and even made descents on the Italian cities, besides stopping the ships which brought wheat from Sicily and Alexandria to feed the Romans.

To enable Pompeius to crush them, authority was given him for three years over all the Mediterranean and fifty miles inland all round, which was nearly the same thing as the whole empire. He divided the sea into thirteen commands, and sent a party to fight the pirates in each; and this was done so effectually, that in forty days they were all hunted out of the west end of the gulf, whither he pursued them with his whole force, beat them in a sea-fight, and then besieged them; but, as he was known to be a just and merciful man, they came to terms with him, and he scattered them about in small colonies in distant cities, so that they might cease to be mischievous.

COAST OF TYRE.

In the meantime, the war with Mithridates had broken out again, and Lucius Lucullus, who had been consul after Pompeius, was fighting with him in the East; but Lucullus did not please the Romans, though he met with good success, and had pushed Mithridates so hard that there was nothing left for Pompeius but to complete the conquest, and he drove the old king beyond Caucasus, and then marched into Syria, where he overthrew the last of the Seleucian kings, Antiochus, and gave him the little kingdom of Commagene to spend the remainder of his life in, while Syria and Phoenicia were made into a great Roman province.

Under the Maccabees, Palestine had struggled into being independent of Syria, but only by the help of the Romans, who, as usual, tried to ally themselves with small states in order to make an excuse for making war on large ones. There was now a great quarrel between two brothers of the Maccabean family, and one of them, Hyrcanus, came to ask the aid of Pompeius. The Roman army marched into the Holy Land, and, after seizing the whole country, was three months besieging Jerusalem, which, after all, it only took by an attack when the Jews were resting on the Sabbath day. Pompeius insisted on forcing his way into the Holy of Holies, and was very much disappointed to find it empty and dark.

He did not plunder the treasury of the Temple, but the Jews remarked that, from the time of this daring entrance, his prosperity seemed to fail him. Before he left the East, however, old Mithridates, who had taken refuge in the Crimea, had been attacked by his own favorite son, and, finding that his power was gone, had taken poison; but, as his constitution was so fortified by antidotes that it took no effect, he caused one of his slaves to kill him.

The son submitted to the Romans, and was allowed to reign on the Bosphorus; but Pompeius had extended the Roman Empire as far as the Euphrates; for though a few small kings still remained, it was only by suffrance from the Romans, who had gained thirty-nine great cities. Egypt, the Parthian kingdom on the Tigris, and Armenia in the mountains, alone remained free.

While all this was going on in the East, there was a very dangerous plot contrived at Rome by a man named Lucius Sergius Catilina, and seven other good-for-nothing nobles, for arming the mob, even the slaves and gladiators, overthrowing the government, seizing all the offices of state, and murdering all their opponents, after the example first set by Marius and Cinna.

MOUNTAINS OF ARMENIA.

Happily such secrets are seldom kept; one of the plotters told the woman he was in love with, and she told one of the consuls, Marcus Tullius Cicero. Cicero was one of the wisest and best men in Rome, and the one whom we really know the best, for he left a great number of letters to his friends, which show us the real mind of the man. He was of the order of the knights, and had been bred up to be a lawyer and orator, and his speeches came to be the great models of Roman eloquence. He was a man of real conscience, and he most deeply loved Rome and her honor; and though he was both vain and timid, he could put these weaknesses aside for the public good. Before all the Senate he impeached Catilina, showing how fully he knew all that he intended. Nothing could be done to him by law till he had actually committed his crime, and Cicero wanted to show him that all was known, so as to cause him to flee and join his friends outside. Catilina tried to face it out, but all the senators began to cry out against him, and he dashed away in terror, and left the city at night. Cicero announced it the next day in a famous speech, beginning, "He is gone; he has rushed away; he has burst forth." Some of his followers in guilt were left at Rome, and just then some letters were brought to Cicero by some of a tribe of Gauls whom they had invited to help them in the ruin of the Senate. This was positive proof, and Cicero caused the nine worst to be seized, and, having proved their guilt, there was a consultation in the Senate as to their fate. Julius Cæsar wanted to keep them prisoners for life, which he said was worse than death, as that, he believed, would end everything; but all the rest of the Senate were for their death, and they were all strangled, without giving them a chance of defending themselves or appealing to the people. Cicero beheld the execution himself, and then went forth to the crowd, merely saying, "They have lived."

CICERO.

Catilina, meantime, had collected 20,000 men in Italy, but they were not half-armed, and the newly-returned proconsul, Metellus, made head against him; while the other consul, Caius Antonius, was recalled from Macedonia with his army. As he was a friend of Catilina, he did not choose to fight with him, and gave up the command to his lieutenant, by whom the wretch was defeated and slain. His head was cut off and sent to Rome.

COLOSSAL STATUE OF POMPEIUS OF THE PALAZZO SPADA AT ROME.

CHAPTER XXVII.
POMPEIUS AND CÆSAR.
61-48.

Pompeius was coming home for his triumph, every one had hopes from him, for things were in a very bad state. There had been a great disturbance at Julius Cæsar's house. Every year there was a festival in honor of Cybele, the Bona Dea, or Good Goddess, to which none but women were admitted, and where it was sacrilege for a man to be seen. In the midst of this feast in Cæsar's house, a slave girl told his mother Aurelia that there was a man among the ladies. Aurelia shut the doors, took a torch and ran through the house, looking in every one's face for the offender, who was found to be Publius Clodius, a worthless young man, who had been in Catilina's conspiracy, but had given evidence against him. He escaped, but was brought to trial, and then borrowed money enough of Crassus the rich, to bribe the judges and avoid the punishment he deserved. Cæsar's wife, the sister of Pompeius was free of blame in the matter, but he divorced her, saying that Cæsar's wife must be free from all suspicion; and this, of course, did not bring her brother home in a friendly spirit to Cæsar.

Pompeius' triumph was the most magnificent that had ever yet been seen. It lasted two days, and the banners that were carried in the procession, bore the names of nine hundred cities and one thousand fortresses which he had conquered.

All the treasures of Mithridates — statues, jewels, and splendid ornaments of gold and silver worked with precious stones — were carried along; and it was reckoned that he had brought home 20,000 talents — equal to £5,000,000 — for the treasury. He was admired, too, for refusing any surname taken from his conquests, and only wearing the laurel wreath of a victor in the Senate.

POMPEIUS.

Pompeius and Cæsar were the great rival names at this time. Pompeius' desire was to keep the old framework, and play the part of Sulla as its protector, only without its violence and bloodshed. Cæsar saw that it was impossible that things should go on as they were, and had made up his mind to take the lead and mould them afresh; but this he could not do while Pompeius was looked up to as the last great conqueror. So Cæsar meant to serve his consulate, take some government where he could grow famous and form an army, and then come home and mould everything anew. After a year's service in Spain as proprætor, Cæsar came back and made friends with Pompeius and Crassus, giving his daughter Julia in marriage to Pompeius, and forming what was called a triumvirate, or union of three men. Thus he easily obtained the consulship, and showed himself the friend of the people by bringing in an Agrarian Law for dividing the public lands in Campania among the poorer citizens, not forgetting Pompeius' old soldiers; also taking other measures which might make the Senate recollect that Sulla had foretold that he would be another Marius and more.

After this, he took Gaul as his province, and spent seven years in subduing it bit by bit, and in making two visits to Britain. He might pretty well trust the rotten state of Rome to be ready for his interference when he came back. Clodius had actually dared to bring Cicero to a trial for having put to death the friends of Catilina without allowing them to plead their own cause. Pompeius would not help him, and the people banished him four hundred miles from Rome, when he went to Sicily, where he was very miserable; but his exile only lasted two years, and then better counsels prevailed, and he was brought home by a general vote, and welcomed almost as if it had been a triumph.

Marcus Porcius Cato was as honest and true a man as Cicero, but very rough and stern, so that he was feared and hated; and there were often fierce quarrels in the Senate and Forum, and in one of these Pompeius' robe was sprinkled with blood. On his return home, his young wife Julia thought he had been hurt, and the shock brought on an illness of which she died; thus breaking the link between her husband and father.

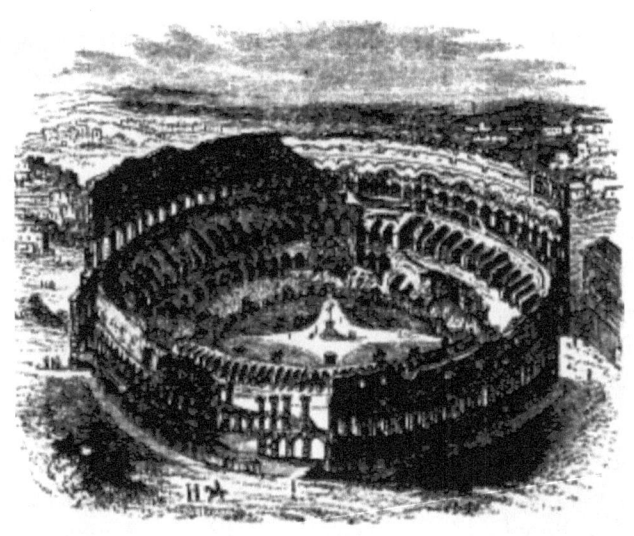

AMPHITHEATRE.

Pompeius did all he could to please the Romans when he was consul together with Crassus. He had been for some time building a most splendid theatre in the Campus Martius, after the Greek fashion, open to the sky, and with tiers of galleries circling round an arena; but the Greeks had never used their theatres for the savage sports for which this was intended. When it was opened, five hundred lions, eighteen elephants, and a multitude of gladiators were provided to fight in different fashions with one another before thirty thousand spectators, the whole being crowned by a temple to Conquering Venus. After his consulate, Pompeius took Spain as his province, but did not go there, managing it by deputy; while Crassus had Syria, and there went to war with the wild Parthians on the Eastern border. In the battle of Carrhæ, the army of Crassus was entirely routed by the Parthians; he was killed, his head was cut off, and his mouth filled up with molten gold in scorn of his riches. At Rome, there was such distress that no one thought much even of such a disaster. Bribes were given to secure elections, and there was nothing but tumult and uproar, in which good men like Cicero and Cato could do nothing. Clodius was killed in one of these frays, and the mob grew so furious that the Senate chose Pompeius to be sole consul to put them down; and this he did for a short time, but all fell into confusion again while he was very ill of a fever at Naples, and even when he recovered there was a feeling that Cæsar was wanted. But Cæsar's friends said he must not be called upon to give up his army unless Pompeius gave up his command of the army in Spain, and neither of them would resign.

Cæsar advanced with all his forces as far as Ravenna, which was still part of Cisalpine Gaul, and then the consul, Marcus Marcellus, begged Pompeius to protect the commonwealth, and he took up arms.

Two of Cæsars great friends, Marcus Antonius and Caius Cassius, who were tribunes, forbade this; and when they were not heeded, they fled to Cæsar's camp asking his protection.

THE ARENA.

So he advanced. It was not lawful for an imperator, or general in command of an army, to come within the Roman territory with his troops except for his triumph, and the little river Rubicon was the boundary of Cisalpine Gaul. So when Cæsar crossed it, he took the first step in breaking through old Roman rules, and thus the saying arose that one has passed the Rubicon when one has gone so far in a matter that there is no turning back. Though Cæsar's army was but small, his fame was such that everybody seemed struck with dismay, even Pompeius himself, and instead of fighting, he carried off all the senators of his party to the South, even to the extreme point of Italy at Brundusium. Cæsar marched after them thither, having met with no resistance, and having, indeed, won all Italy in sixty days. As he advanced on Brundusium, Pompeius embarked on board a ship in the harbor and sailed away, meaning, no doubt, to raise an army in the provinces and return — some feared like Sulla — to take vengeance.

Cæsar was appointed Dictator, and after crushing Pompeius' friends in Spain, he pursued him into Macedonia, where Pompeius had been collecting all the friends of the old commonwealth. There was a great battle fought at Pharsalia, a battle which nearly put an end to the old government of Rome, for Cæsar gained a great victory; and Pompeius fled to the coast, where he found a vessel and sailed for Egypt. He sent a message to ask shelter at Alexandria, and the advisers of the young king pretended to welcome him, but they really intended to make friends with the victor; and as Pompeius stepped ashore he was stabbed in the back, his body thrown into the surf, and his head cut off.

CHAPTER XXVIII.
JULIUS CÆSAR.
48 — 44.

With Pompeius fell the hopes of those who were faithful to the old government, such as Cicero and Cato. They had only to wait and see what Cæsar would do, and with the memory of Marius in their minds.

JULIUS CÆSAR.

Cæsar did not come at once to Rome; he had first to reduce the East to obedience. Egypt was under the last descendants of Alexander's general Ptolemy, and was an ally of Rome, that is, only remaining a kingdom by her permission. The king was a wretched weak lad; his sister Cleopatra, who was joined with him in the throne, was one of the most beautiful and winning women who ever lived. Cæsar, who needed money, demanded some that was owing to the state. The young king's advisers refused, and Cæsar, who had but a small force with him, was shut up in a quarter of Alexandria where he could get no fresh water but from pits which his men dug in the sand. He burnt the Egyptian fleet that it might not stop the succors that were coming from Syria, and he tried to take the Isle of Pharos, with the lighthouse on it, but his ship was sunk, and he was obliged to save himself by swimming, holding his journals in one hand above the water. However, the forces from Syria were soon brought to him, and he was able to fight a battle in which the young king was drowned; and Egypt was at his mercy. Cleopatra was determined to have an interview with him, and had herself carried into his rooms in a roll of carpet, and when there, she charmed him so much that he set her up as queen of Egypt. He remained three months longer in Egypt collecting money; and hearing that Pharnaces, the son of Mithridates, had attacked the Roman settlements in Asia Minor, he sailed for Tarsus, marched against Pharnaces, routed and killed him in battle. The success was announced to the Senate in the following brief words, "*Veni, vidi, vici*" — "I came, I saw, I conquered."

He was a second time appointed Dictator, and came home to arrange affairs; but there were no proscriptions, though he took away the estates of those who opposed him. There was still a party of the senators and their supporters who had followed Pompeius in Africa, with Cato and Cnæus Pompeius, the eldest son of the great leader, and Cæsar had to follow them thither. He gave them a great defeat at Thapsus, and the remnant took refuge in the city of Utica, whither Cæsar followed them.

CATO.

They would have stood a siege, but the townspeople would not consent, and Cato sent off all his party by sea, and remained alone with his son and a few of his friends, not to face the conqueror, but to die by his own sword ere he came, as the Romans had learned from Stoic philosophy to think the nobler part.

Such of the Senate as had not joined Pompeius were ready to fall down and worship Cæsar when he came home. So rejoiced was Rome to fear no proscription, that temples were dedicated to Cæsar's clemency, and his image was to be carried in procession with those of the gods.

FUNERAL SOLEMNITIES IN THE COLUMBARIUM (lit. Pigeon-house) OF THE HOUSE OF JULIUS CÆSAR AT THE PORTA CAPENA IN ROME.
(The rows of niches for the cinerary urns in a Roman sepulchre were called by this name from their resemblance to a dovecot.)

He was named Dictator for ten years, and was received with four triumphs — over the Gauls, over the Egyptians, over Pharnaces, and over Juba, an African king who had aided Cato. Foremost of the Gaulish prisoners was the brave Vercingetorix, and among the Egyptians, Arsinoë, the sister of Cleopatra. A banquet was given at his cost to the whole Roman people, and the shows of gladiators and beasts surpassed all that had ever been seen. The Julii were said to be descended from Æneas and to Venus, as his ancestress, Cæsar dedicated a breastplate of pearls from the river mussels of Britain. Still, however, he had to go to Spain to reduce the sons of Pompeius. They were defeated in battle, the elder was killed, but Cnæus, the younger, held out in the mountains and hid himself among the natives.

After this, Cæsar returned to Rome to carry out his plans. He was dictator for ten years and consul for five, and was also imperator or commander of an army he was not made to disband, so that he nearly was as powerful as any king; and, as he saw that such an enormous domain as Rome now possessed could never be governed by two magistrates changing every year, he prepared matters for there being one ruler. The influence of the Senate, too, he weakened very much by naming a great many persons to it of no rank or distinction, till there were nine hundred members, and nobody thought much of being a senator. He also made an immense number of new citizens, and he caused a great survey to be begun by Roman officers in preparation for properly arranging the provinces, governments, and tribute; and he began to have the laws drawn up in regular order. In fact, he was one of the greatest men the world has ever produced, not only as a conqueror, but a statesman and ruler; and though his power over Rome was not according to the laws, and had been gained by a rebellion, he was using it for her good.

He was learned in all philosophy and science, and his history of his wars in Gaul has come down to our times. As a high patrician by birth, he was Pontifex Maximus, or chief priest, and thus had to fix all the festival days in each year. Now the year had been supposed to be only three hundred and fifty-five days long, and the Pontifex put in another month or several days whenever he pleased, so that there was great confusion, and the feast days for the harvest and vintage came, according to the calendar, three months before there was any corn or grapes.

To set this to rights, since it was now understood that the length of the year was three hundred and sixty-five days and six hours, Cæsar and the scientific men who assisted him devised the fresh arrangement that we call leap year, adding a day to the three hundred and sixty-five once in four years. He also changed the name of one of the summer months from Sextile to July, in honor of himself. Another work of his was restoring Corinth and Carthage, which had both been ruined the same year, and now were both refounded the same year.

He was busy about the glory of the state, but there was much to shock old Roman feelings in his conduct. Cleopatra had followed him to Rome, and he was thinking of putting away his wife Calphurnia to marry her. But his keeping the dictatorship was the real grievance, and the remains of the old party in the Senate could not bear that the patrician freedom of Rome should be lost. Every now and then his flatterers offered him a royal crown and hailed him as king, though he always refused it, and this title still stirred up bitter hatred. He was preparing an army, intending to march into the further East, avenge Crassus' defeat on the Parthians, and march where no one but Alexander had made his way; and if he came back victorious from thence, nothing would be able to stand against him.

The plotters then resolved to strike before he set out. Caius Cassius, a tall, lean man, who had lately been made prætor, was the chief conspirator, and with him was Marcus Junius Brutus, a descendant of him who overthrew the Tarquins, and husband to Porcia, Cato's daughter, also another Brutus named Decimus, hitherto a friend of Cæsar, and newly appointed to the government of Cisalpine Gaul. These and twelve more agreed to murder Cæsar on the 15th of March, called in the Roman calendar the Ides of March, when he went to the senate-house.

Rumors got abroad and warnings came to him about that special day. His wife dreamt so terrible a dream that he had almost yielded to her entreaties to stay at home, when Decimus Brutus came in and laughed him out of it. As he was carried to the senate-house in a litter, a man gave him a writing and begged him to read it instantly; but he kept it rolled in his hand without looking. As he went up the steps he said to the augur Spurius, "The Ides of March are come." "Yes, Cæsar," was the answer; "but they are not passed." A few steps further on, one of the conspirators met him with a petition, and the others joined in it, clinging to his robe and his neck, till another caught his toga and pulled it over his arms, and then the first blow was struck with a dagger. Cæsar struggled at first as all fifteen tried to strike at him, but, when he saw the hand uplifted of his treacherous friend Decimus, he exclaimed, "*Et tu Brute*" — "Thou, too, Brutus" — drew his toga over his head, and fell dead at the foot of the statue of Pompeius.

CHAPTER XXIX.
THE SECOND TRIUMVIRATE.
44 — 33.

The murderers of Cæsar had expected the Romans to hail them as deliverers from a tyrant, but his great friend Marcus Antonius, who was, together with him, consul for that year, made a speech over his body as it lay on a couch of gold and ivory in the Forum ready for the funeral. Antonius read aloud Cæsar's will, and showed what benefits he had intended for his fellow-citizens, and how he loved them, so that love for him and wrath against his enemies filled every hearer. The army, of course, were furious against the murderers; the Senate was terrified, and granted everything Antonius chose to ask, provided he would protect them, whereupon he begged for a guard for himself that he might be saved from Cæsar's fate, and this they gave him; while the fifteen murderers fled secretly, mostly to Cisalpine Gaul, of which Decimus Brutus was governor.

Cæsar had no child but the Julia who had been wife to Pompeius, and his heir was his young cousin Caius Octavius, who changed his name to Caius Julius Cæsar Octavianus, and, coming to Rome, demanded his inheritance, which Antonius had seized, declaring that it was public money; but Octavianus, though only eighteen, showed so much prudence and fairness that many of the Senate were drawn towards him rather than Antonius, who had always been known as a bad, untrustworthy man; but the first thing to be done was to put down the murderers — Decimus Brutus was in Gaul, Marcus Brutus and Cassius in Macedonia, and Sextus Pompeius had also raised an army in Spain.

Good men in the Senate dreaded no one so much as Antonius, and put their hope in young Octavianus. Cicero made a set of speeches against Antonius, which are called Philippics, because they denounce him as Demosthenes used to denounce Philip of Macedon, and like them, too, they were the last flashes of spirit in a sinking state; and Cicero, in those days, was the foremost and best man who was trying at his own risk to save the old institutions of his country. But it was all in vain; they were too rotten to last, and there were not enough of honest men to make a stand against a violent unscrupulous schemer like Antonius, above all now that the clever young Octavianus saw it was for his interest to make common cause with him, and with a third friend of Cæsar, rich but dull, named Marcus Æmilius Lepidus. They called on Decimus Brutus to surrender his forces to them, and marched against him. Then his troops deserted him, and he tried to escape into the Alps, but was delivered up to Antonius and put to death.

MARCUS ANTONIUS.

Soon after, Antonius, Lepidus, and Octavianus all met on a little island in the river Rhenus and agreed to form a triumvirate for five years for setting things to rights once more, all three enjoying consular power together; and, as they had the command of all the armies, there was no one to stop them. Lepidus was to stay and govern Rome, while the other two hunted down the murderers of Cæsar in the East. But first, there was a deadly vengeance to be taken in the city upon all who could be supposed to have favored the murder of Cæsar, or who could be enemies to their schemes. So these three sat down with a list of the citizens before them to make a proscription, each letting a kinsman or friend of his own be marked for death, provided he might slay one related to another of the three. The dreadful list was set up in the Forum, and a price paid for the heads of the people in it, so that soldiers, ruffians, and slaves brought them in; but it does not seem that — as in the other two proscriptions — there was random murder, and many bribed their assassins and escaped from Italy. Octavianus had marked the fewest and tried to save Cicero, but Antonius insisted on his death. On hearing that he was in the fatal roll, Cicero had left Rome with his brother, and slowly travelled towards the coast from one country house to another till he came to Antium, whence he meant to sail for Greece; but there he was overtaken. His brother was killed at once, but he was put into a boat by his slaves, and went down the coast to Formiæ, where he landed again, and, going to a house near, said he would rather die in his own country which he had so often saved. However, when the pursuers knocked at the gate, his slaves placed him in a litter and hurried him out at another door. He was, however, again overtaken, and he forbade his slaves to fight for him, but stretched out his throat for the sword, with his eyes full upon it. His head was carried to Antonius, whose wife Fulvia actually pierced the tongue with her bodkin in revenge for the speeches it had made against her husband.

After this dreadful work, Antonius and Octavianus went across to Greece, where Marcus Brutus had collected the remains of the army that had fought under Pompeius. He had been made much of at Athens, where his statue had been set up beside that of Harmodius and Aristogeiton, the slayers of Pisistratus. Cassius had plundered Asia Minor, and the two met at Sardis. It is said that the night before they were to pass into Macedonia, Brutus was sitting alone in his tent, when he saw the figure of a man before him. "Who art thou?" he asked, and the answer was, "I am thine evil genius, Brutus; I will meet thee again at Philippi."

MARCUS BRUTUS.

And it was at Philippi that Brutus and Cassius found themselves face to face with Antonius and Octavianus. Each army was divided into two, and Brutus, who fought against Octavianus, put his army to flight, but Cassius was driven back by Antonius; and seeing a troop of horsemen coming towards him, he thought all was lost, and threw himself upon a sword. Brutus gathered the troops together, and after twenty days renewed the fight, when he was routed, fled, and hid himself, but after some hours put himself to death, as did his wife Porcia when she heard of his end.

After this, Octavianus went back to Italy, while Antonius stayed to pacify the East. When he was at Tarsus, the lovely queen of Egypt came, resolved to win him over. She sailed up the Cydnus in a beautiful galley, carved, gilded, and inlaid with ivory, with sails of purple silk and silvered oars, moving to the sound of flutes, while she lay on the deck under a star-spangled canopy arrayed as Venus, with her ladies as nymphs, and little boys as Cupids fanning her. Antonius was perfectly fascinated, and she took him back to Alexandria with her, heeding nothing but her and the delights with which she entertained him, though his wife Fulvia and his brother were struggling to keep up his power at Rome. He did come home, but only to make a fresh agreement with Octavianus, by which Fulvia was given up and he married Octavia, the widow of Marcellus and sister of Octavianus. But he could not bear to stay long away from Cleopatra, and, deserting Octavia, he returned to Egypt, where the most wonderful revelries were kept up. Stories are told of eight wild boars being roasted in one day, each being begun a little later than the last, that one might be in perfection when Antonius should call for his dinner. Cleopatra vowed once that she would drink the most costly of draughts, and, taking off an earring of inestimable price, dissolved it in vinegar and swallowed it.

ALEXANDRIA.

In the meantime, Octavianus and Lepidus together had put down Decimus, and Lepidus had then tried to overcome Octavianus, but was himself conquered and banished; for Octavianus, was a kindly man, who never shed blood if he could help it, and, now that he was alone at Rome, won every one's heart by his gracious ways, while Antonius' riots in Egypt were a scandal to all who loved virtue and nobleness. So far was the Roman fallen that he even promised Cleopatra to conquer Italy and make Alexandria the capital of the world. Octavia tried to win him back, but she was a grave, virtuous Roman matron, and coarse, dissipated Antonius did not care for her compared with the enticing Egyptian queen. It was needful at last for Octavianus to destroy this dangerous power, and he mustered a fleet and army, while Antonius and Cleopatra sailed out of Alexandria with their ships and gave battle off the Cape of Actium. In the midst, either fright or treachery made Cleopatra sail away, and all the Egyptian ships with her, so that Antonius turned at once and fled with her. They tried to raise the East in their favor, but all their allies deserted them, and their soldiers went over to Alexandria, where Octavianus followed them. Then Cleopatra betrayed her lover, and put into the hands of Octavianus the ships in which he might have fled. He killed himself, and Cleopatra surrendered, hoping to charm young Octavianus as she had done Julius and Antonius, but when she saw him grave and unmoved, and found he meant to exhibit her in his triumph, she went to the tomb of Antonius and crowned it with flowers. The next day she was found on her couch, in her royal robes, dead, and her two maids dying too. "Is this well?" asked the man who found her. "It is well for the daughter of kings," said her maid with her last breath. Cleopatra had long made experiments on easy ways of death, and it was believed that an asp was brought to her in a basket of figs as the means of her death.

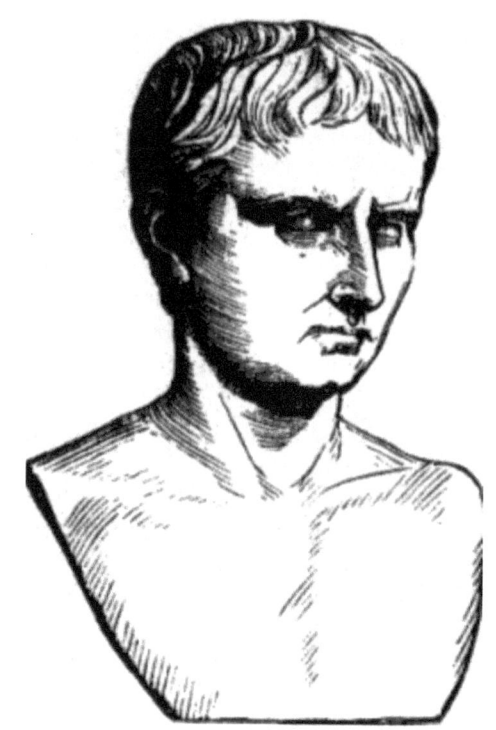

CAIUS OCTAVIUS.

CHAPTER XXX.
CÆSAR AUGUSTUS.B.C. 33 – A.D. 14.

The death of Antonius ended the fierce struggles which had torn Rome so long. Octavianus was left alone; all the men who had striven for the old government were dead, and those who were left were worn out and only longed for rest. They had found that he was kind and friendly, and trusted to him thankfully, nay, were ready to treat him as a kind of god. The old frame of constitution went on as usual; there was still a Senate, still consuls, and all the other magistrates, but Cæsar Octavianus had the power belonging to each gathered in one. He was prince of the Senate, which gave him rule in the city; prætor, which made him judge, and gave him a special guard of soldiers called the Prætorian Guard to execute justice; and tribune of the people, which made him their voice; and even after his triumph he was still imperator, or general of the army. This word becomes in English, emperor, but it meant at this time merely commander-in-chief. He was also Pontifex Maximus, as Julius Cæsar had been; and there was a general feeling that he was something sacred and set apart as the ruler and peace-maker; and, as he shared this feeling himself, he took the name of Augustus, which is the one by which he is always known.

He did not, however, take to himself any great show or state. He lived in his family abode, and dressed and walked about the streets like any other Roman gentleman of consular rank, and no special respect was paid to him in speech, for, warned by the fate of Julius, he was determined to prevent the Romans from being put in mind of kings and crowns.

STATUE OF AUGUSTUS AT THE VATICAN.

He was a wise and deep-thinking man, and he tried to carry out the plans of Julius for the benefit of the nation and of the whole Roman world. He had the survey finished of all the countries of the empire, which now formed a complete border round the Mediterranean Sea, reaching as far north as the British Channel, the Alps, and the Black Sea; as far south as the African desert, as far west as the Atlantic, and east as the borders of the Euphrates; and he also had a universal census made of the whole of the inhabitants. It was the first time such a thing had been possible, for all the world was at last at peace, so that the Temple of Janus was closed for the third and last time in Roman history. There was a feeling all over the world that a great Deliverer and peaceful Prince was to be expected at this time. One of the Sybils was believed to have so sung, and the Romans, in their relief at the good rule of Augustus, thought he was the promised one; but they little knew why God had brought about this great stillness from all wars, or why He moved the heart of Augustus to make the decree that all the world should be taxed — namely, that the true Prince of Peace, the real Deliverer, might be born in the home of His forefathers, Bethlehem, the city of David.

The purpose of Augustus' taxing was to make a regular division of the empire into provinces for the proconsuls to govern, with lesser divisions for the proprætors, while many cities, especially Greek ones, were allowed their own magistrates, and some small tributary kingdoms still remained till the old royal family should either die out or offend the Romans. In these lands the people were governed by their own laws, unless they were made Roman citizens; and this freedom was more and more granted, and saved them from paying the tribute all the rest had to pay, and which went to support the armies and other public institutions at Rome, and to provide the corn which was regularly distributed to such citizens as claimed it at Rome. A Roman colony was a settlement, generally of old soldiers who had had lands granted to them, and kept their citizenship; and it was like another little Rome managing its own affairs, though subject to the mother city. There were many of these colonies, especially in Gaul on the north coast, to defend it from the Germans. Cologne was one, and still keeps its name. The tribute was carefully fixed, and Augustus did his best to prevent the governors from preying on the people.

He tried to bring back better ways to Rome, which was in a sad state, full of vice and riot, and with little of the old, noble, hardy ways of the former times. The educated men had studied Greek philosophy till they had no faith in their own gods, and, indeed, had so mixed up their mythology with the Greek that they really did not know who their own were, and could not tell who were the greater gods whom Decius Mus invoked before he rushed on the enemy; and yet they kept up their worship, because their feasts were so connected with the State that everything depended on them; but they made them no real judges or helpers. The best men of the time were those who had taken up the Stoic philosophy, which held that virtue was above all things, whether it was rewarded or not; the worst were often the Epicureans, who held that we had better enjoy all we can in this life, being sure of nothing else.

Learning was much esteemed in the time of Augustus. He and his two great friends, Caius Cilnius Mæcenas and Vipsanius Agrippa, both had a great esteem for scholarship and poetry, and in especial the house of Mæcenas was always open to literary men. The two chief poets of Rome, Publius Virgilius Maro and Quintus Horatius Flaccus, were warm friends of his. Virgil wrote poems on husbandry, and short dialogue poems called eclogues, in one of which he spoke of the time of Augustus in words that would almost serve as a prophecy of the kingdom of Him who was just born at Bethlehem. By desire of Augustus, he also wrote the *Æneid*, a poem on the war-doings of Æneas and his settlement in Italy.

Horace wrote odes and letters in verse and satires, which show the habits and ways of thinking of his time in a very curious manner; and there were many other writers whose works have not come down to us; but the Latin of this time is the model of the language, and an Augustan age has ever since been a term for one in which literature flourishes.

All the early part of Augustus' reign was prosperous, but he had no son, only a daughter named Julia. He meant to marry her to Marcellus, the son of his sister Antonia, but Marcellus died young, and was lamented in Virgil's *Æneid*; so Julia was given to

Agrippa's son. Augustus' second wife was Livia, who had been married to Tiberius Claudius Nero, and had two sons, Tiberius and Drusus, whom Augustus adopted as his own and intended for his heirs; and when Julia lost her husband Agrippa and her two young sons, he forced Tiberius to divorce the young wife he really loved to marry her. It was a great grief to Tiberius, and seems to have quite changed his character into being grave, silent, and morose. Julia, though carefully brought up, was one of the most wicked and depraved of women, and almost broke her father's heart. He banished her to an island near Rhegium, and when she died there, would allow no funeral honors to be paid to her.

PAINTINGS IN THE HOUSE OF LIVIA.

The peace was beginning to be broken by wars with the Germans; and young Drusus was commanding the army against them, and gaining such honor that he was called Germanicus, when he fell from his horse and died of his injuries, leaving one young son. He was buried at Rome, and his brother Tiberius walked all the way beside the bier, with his long flaxen hair flowing on his shoulders. Tiberius then went back to command the armies on the Rhine. Some half-conquered country lay beyond, and the Germans in the forests were at this time under a brave leader called Arminius. They were attacked by the proconsul Quinctilius Varus, and near the river Ems, in the Herycimian forest, Arminius turned on him and routed him completely, cutting off the whole army, so that only a few fled back to Tiberius to tell the tale, and he had to fall back and defend the Rhine.

The news of this disaster was a terrible shock to the Emperor. He sat grieving over it, and at times he dashed his head against the wall, crying, "Varus, Varus! give me back my legions." His friends were dead, he was an old man now, and sadness was around him. He was soon, however, grave and composed again; and, as his health began to fail, he sent for Tiberius and put his affairs into his hands. When his dying day came, he met it calmly. He asked if there was any fear of a tumult on his death, and was told there was none; then he called for a mirror, and saw that his grey hair and beard were in order, and, asking his friends whether he had played his part well, he uttered a verse from a play bidding them applaud his exit, bade Livia remember him, and so died in his seventy-seventh year, having ruled fifty-eight years — ten as a triumvir, forty-eight alone.

CHAPTER XXXI.
TIBERIUS AND CALIGULA.
A.D. 14 — 41.

No difficulty was made about giving all the powers Augustus had held to his stepson, Tiberius Claudius Nero, who had also a right to the names of Julius Cæsar Augustus, and was in his own time generally called Cæsar. The Senate had grown too helpless to think for themselves, and all the choice they ever made of the consuls was that the Emperor gave out four names, among which they chose two.

Tiberius had been a grave, morose man ever since he was deprived of the wife he loved, and had lost his brother; and he greatly despised the mean, cringing ways round him, and kept to himself; but his nephew, called Germanicus, after his father, was the person whom every one loved and trusted. He had married Agrippina, Julia's daughter, who was also a very good and noble person; and when he was sent against the Germans, she went with him, and her little boys ran about among the soldiers, and were petted by them. One of them, Caius, was called by the soldiers Caligula, or the Little Shoe, because he wore a caliga or shoe like theirs; and he never lost the nickname.

Germanicus earned his surname over again by driving Arminius back; but he was more enterprising than would have been approved by Augustus, who thought it wiser to guard what he had than to make wider conquests; and Tiberius was not only one of the same mind, but was jealous of the great love that all the army were showing for his nephew, and this distrust was increased when the soldiers in the East begged for Germanicus to lead them against the Parthians. He set out, visiting all the famous places in Greece by the way, and going to see the wonders of Egypt, but while in Syria he fell ill of a wasting sickness and died, so that many suspected the spy, Cnæus Piso, whom Tiberius had sent with him, of having poisoned him. When his wife Agrippina came home, bringing his corpse to be burnt and his ashes placed in the burying-place of the Cæsars, there was universal love and pity for her. Piso seized on all the offices that

Germanicus had held, but was called back to Rome, and was just going to be put upon his trial when he cut his own throat.

RUINS OF THE PALACES OF TIBERIUS.

All this tended to make Tiberius more gloomy and distrustful, and when his mother Livia died he had no one to keep him in check, but fell under the influence of a man named Sejanus, who managed all his affairs for him, while he lived in a villa in the island of Capreæ in the Bay of Naples, seeing hardly any but a few intimates, given up to all sorts of evil luxuries and self-indulgences, and hating and dreading every one. Agrippina was so much loved and respected that he dreaded and disliked her beyond all others; and Sejanus contrived to get up an accusation of plotting against the state, upon which she and her eldest son were banished to two small rocky isles in the Mediterranean Sea. The other two sons, Drusus and Caius, were kept by Tiberius at Capreæ, till Tiberius grew suspicious of Drusus and threw him into prison. Sejanus, who had encouraged all his dislike to his own kinsmen, and was managing all Rome, then began to hope to gain the full power; but his plans were guessed by Tiberius, and he caused his former favorite to be set upon in the senate-house and put to death.

AGRIPPINA.

It is strange to remember that, while such dark deeds were being done at Rome, came the three years when the true Light was shining in the darkness. It was in the time of Tiberius Cæsar, when Pontius Pilatus was proprætor of Palestine, that our Lord Jesus Christ spent three years in teaching and working miracles; then was crucified and slain by wicked hands, that the sin of mankind might be redeemed. Then He rose again from the dead and ascended into Heaven, leaving His Apostles to make known what he had done in all the world.

To the East, where our Lord dwelt, nay, to all the rest of the empire, the reign of Tiberius was a quiet time, with the good government arranged by Augustus working on. It was only his own family, and the senators and people of rank at Rome, who had much to fear from his strange, harsh, and jealous temper. The Claudian family had in all times been shy, proud, and stern, and to have such power as belonged to Augustus Cæsar was more than their heads could bear. Tiberius hated and suspected everybody, and yet he did not like putting people to death, so he let Drusus be starved to death in his prison, and Agrippina chose the same way of dying in her island, while some of the chief senators received such messages that they put themselves to death. He led a wretched life, watching for treason and fearing everybody, and trying to drown the thought of danger in the banquets of Capreæ, where the remains of his villa may still be seen. Once he set out, intending to visit Rome, but no sooner had he landed in Campania than the sight of hundreds of country people shouting welcome so disturbed him that he hastened on board ship again, and thus entered the Tiber; but at the very sight of the hills of Rome his terror returned, and he had his galley turned about and went back to his island, which he never again quitted.

Only two males of his family were left now — a great-nephew and a nephew, Caius, that son of the second Germanicus who had been nicknamed Caligula, a youth of a strange, exciteable, feverish nature, but who from his fright at Tiberius had managed to keep the peace with him, and had only once been for a short time in disgrace; and his uncle, the youngest son of the first Germanicus, commonly called Claudius, a very dull, heavy man, fond of books, but so slow and shy that he was considered to be wanting in brains, and thus had never fallen under suspicion.

At length Tiberius fell ill, and when he was known to be dying, he was smothered with pillows as he began to recover from a fainting fit, lest he should take vengeance on those who had for a moment thought him dead. He died A.D. 37, and the power went to Caligula, properly called Caius, who was only twenty-five, and who began in a kindly, generous spirit, which pleased the people and gave them hope; but to have so much power was too much for his brain, and he can only be thought of as mad, especially after he had a severe illness, which made the people so anxious that he was puffed up with the notion of his own importance.

ROME IN THE TIME OF AUGUSTUS CÆSAR.

He put to death all who offended him, and, inheriting some of Tiberius' distrust and hatred of the people, he cried out, when they did not admire one of his shows as much as he expected, "Would that the people of Rome had but one neck, so that I might behead them all at once." He planned great public buildings, but had not steadiness to carry them out; and he became so greedy of the fame which, poor wretch, he could not earn, that he was jealous even of the dead. He burned the books of Livy and Virgil out of the libraries, and deprived the statues of the great men of old of the marks by which they were known — Cincinnatus of his curls, and Torquatus of his collar, and he forbade the last of the Pompeii to be called Magnus.

He made an expedition into Gaul, and talked of conquering Britain, but he got no further than the shore of the channel, where, instead of setting sail, he bade the soldiers gather up shells, which he sent home to the Senate to be placed among the treasures of the Capitol, calling them the spoils of the conquered ocean. Then he collected the German slaves and the tallest Gauls he could find, commanded the latter to dye their hair and beards to a light color, and brought them home to walk in his triumph. The Senate, however, were slow to understand that he could really expect a triumph, and this affronted him so much that, when they offered him one, he would not have it, and went on insulting them. He made his horse a consul, though only for a day, and showed it with golden oats before it in a golden manger. Once, when the two consuls were sitting by him, he burst out laughing, to think, he said, how with one word he could make both their heads roll on the floor.

The provinces were not so ill off, but the state of Rome was unbearable. Everybody was in danger, and at last a plot was formed for his death; and as he was on his way from his house to the circus, and stopped to look at some singers who were going to perform, a party of men set upon him and killed him with many wounds, after he had reigned only five years, and when he was but thirty years old.

CHAPTER XXXII.
CLAUDIUS AND NERO.
A.D. 41-68.

Poor dull Claudius heard an uproar and hid himself, thinking he was going to be murdered like his nephew, but still worse was going to befall him. They were looking for him to make him Emperor, for he was the last of his family. He was clumsy in figure, though his face was good, and he was a kind-hearted man, who made large promises, and tried to do well; but he was slow and timid, and let himself be led by wicked men and women, so that his rule ended no better than that of the former Cæsars.

He began in a spirited way, by sending troops who conquered the southern part of Britain, and making an expedition thither himself. His wife chose to share his triumph, which was not, as usual, a drive in a chariot, but a sitting in armor on their thrones, with the eagles and standards over their heads, and the prisoners led up before them. Among them came the great British chief Caractacus, who is said to have declared that he could not think why those who had such palaces as there were at Rome should want the huts of the Britons.

Claudius was kind to the people in the distant provinces. He gave the Jews a king again, Herod Agrippa, the grandson of the first Herod, who was much loved by them, but died suddenly after a few years at Cæsarea, after the meeting with the Tyrians, when he let them greet him as a god. There were a great many Jews living at Rome, but those from Jerusalem quarrelled with those from Alexandria; and one year, when there was a great scarcity of corn, Claudius banished them all from Rome.

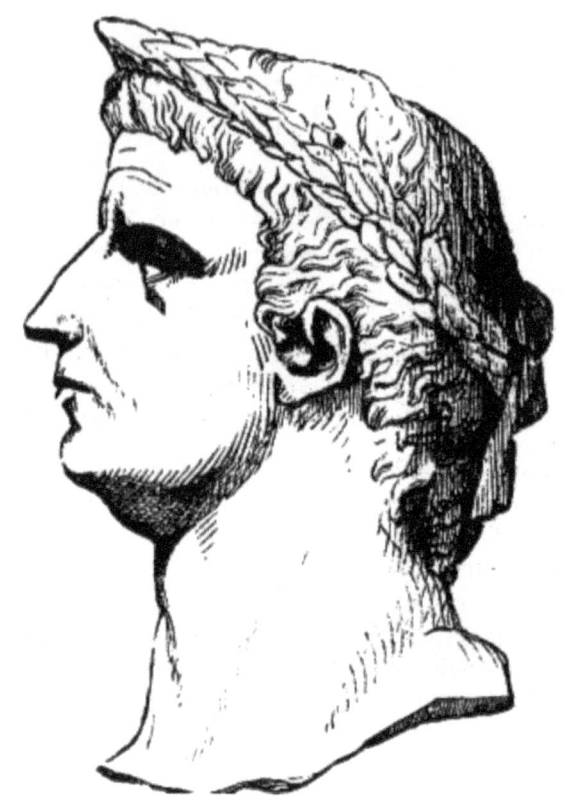

CLAUDIUS.

Claudius was very unhappy in his wives. Two he divorced, and then married a third named Messalina, who was given up to all kinds of wickedness which he never guessed at, while she used all manner of arts to keep up her beauty and to deceive him. At last she actually married a young man while Claudius was absent from Rome; but when this came to his knowledge, he had her put to death. His last wife was, however, the worst of all. She was the daughter of the good Germanicus, and bore her mother's name of Agrippina. She had been previously married to Lucius Domitius Ænobarbus, by whom she had a son, whom Claudius adopted when he married her, though he had a child of his own called Britannicus, son to Messalina. Romans had never married their nieces before, but the power of the Emperors was leading them to trample down all law and custom, and it was for the misfortune of Claudius that he did so in this case, for Agrippina's purpose was to put every one out of the way of her own son, who, taking all the Claudian and Julian names in addition to his own, is commonly known as Nero. She married him to Claudius' daughter Octavia, and then, after much tormenting the Emperor, she poisoned him with a dish of mushrooms, and bribed his physician to take care that he did not recover. He died A.D. 54, and, honest and true-hearted as he had been, the Romans were glad to be rid of him, and told mocking stories of him. Indeed, they were very bad in all ways themselves, and many of the ladies were poisoners like Agrippina, so that the city almost deserved the tyrant who came after Claudius. Nero, the son of Agrippina by her first marriage, and Britannicus, the son of Claudius and Messalina, were to reign together; but Nero was the elder, and as soon as his poor young cousin came to manhood, Agrippina had a dose of poison ready for him.

Nero, however, began well. He had been well brought up by Seneca, an excellent student of the Stoic philosophy, who, with Burrhus, the commander of the Prætorian Guard, guided the young Emperor with good advice through the first five years of his reign; and though his wicked mother called herself Augusta, and had equal honors paid her with her son, not much harm was done to the government till Nero fell in love with a wicked woman, Poppæa Sabina, who was a proverb for vanity, and was said to keep five hundred she-asses that she might bathe in their milk to preserve her complexion. Nero wanted to marry this lady, and as his mother befriended his neglected wife Octavia, he ordered that when she went to her favorite villa at Baiæ her galley should be wrecked, and if she was not drowned, she should be stabbed. Octavia was divorced, sent to an island, and put to death there; and after Nero married Poppæa, he quickly grew more violent and savage.

Burrhus died about the same time, and Seneca alone could not restrain the Emperor from his foolish vanity. He would descend into the arena of the great amphitheatre and sing to the lyre his own compositions; and he showed off his charioteering in the circus before the whole assembled city, letting no one go away till the performance was over. It very much shocked the patricians, but the mob were delighted, and he chiefly cared for their praises. He was building a huge palace, called the Golden House because of its splendid decorations; and, needing money, he caused accusations to be got up against all the richer men that he might have their hoards.

NERO.

A terrible fire broke out in Rome, which raged for six days, and entirely destroyed fourteen quarters of the city. While it was burning, Nero, full of excitement, stood watching it, and sang to his lyre the description of the burning of Troy. A report therefore arose that he had actually caused the fire for the amusement of watching it; and to put this out of men's minds he accused the Christians. The Christian faith had begun to be known in Rome during the last reign, and it was to Nero, as Cæsar, that St. Paul had appealed. He had spent two years in a hired house of his own at Rome, and thus had been in the guard-room of the Prætorians, but he was released after being tried at "Cæsar's judgment-seat," and remained at large until this sudden outburst which caused the first persecution. Then he was taken at Nicopolis, and St. Peter at Rome, and they were thrown into the Mamertine dungeon. Rome counts St. Peter as her first bishop. On the 29th of June, A.D. 66, both suffered; St. Paul, as a Roman citizen, being beheaded with the sword; St. Peter crucified, with his head, by his own desire, downwards. Many others suffered at the same time, some being thrown to the beasts, while others were wrapped in cloths covered with pitch, and slowly burnt to light the games in the Emperor's gardens. At last the people were shocked, and cried out for these horrors to end. And Nero, who cared for the people, turned his hatred and cruelty against men of higher class whose fate they heeded less. So common was it to have a message advising a man to put himself to death rather than be sentenced, that every one had studied easy ways of dying. Nero's old tutor, Seneca, felt his tyranny unbearable, and had joined in a plot for overthrowing him, but it was found out, and Seneca had to die by his own hand. The way he chose, and his wife too for his sake, was to open their veins, get into a warm bath, and bleed to death.

Nero made a journey to Greece, and showed off at Olympus and the Isthmus, at the same time robbing the Greek cities of numbers of their best statues and reliefs to adorn his Golden House; for the Romans had no original art — they could only imitate the Greeks and employ Greek artists. But danger was closing in on Nero. Such an Emperor could be endured no longer, and the generals of the armies in the provinces began to threaten him, they not being smitten dumb and helpless as every one at Rome seemed to be.

The Spanish army, under an officer named Galba, who was seventy-two years old, but to whom Augustus had said when he was a little boy, "You too shall share my taste of empire," began to move homewards to attack the tyrant, and the army from Gaul advanced to join it. Nero went nearly wild with fright, sometimes raging, sometimes tearing his hair and clothes; and the people began to turn against him in anger at a dearth of corn, saying he spent everything on his own pleasures. As Galba came nearer, the nobles and knights hoped for deliverance, and the Prætorian Guard showed that they meant to join their fellow-soldiers, and would not fight for him. The wretched Emperor found himself alone, and vainly called for some one to kill him, for he had not nerve to do it himself. He fled to a villa in the country, and wandered in the woods till he heard that, if he was caught, he would be put to death in the "ancient fashion," which he was told was being fixed with his neck in a forked stick and beaten to death. Then, hearing the hoofs of the horses of his pursuers, he set a sword against his breast and made a slave drive it home, and was groaning his last when the horsemen came up. He was but 30 years old, and was the last Emperor who could trace any connection, even by adoption, with Augustus. He perished A.D. 68.

CHAPTER XXXIII.
THE FLAVIAN FAMILY.
62-96.

The ablest of all Nero's officers was Titus Flavius Vespasianus, a stern, rigid old soldier, who, with his son of the same name, was in the East, preparing to put down a great rising of the Jews. He waited to see what was going to happen, and in a very few weeks old Galba had offended the soldiers by his saving ways; there was a rising against him, and another soldier named Otho became Emperor; but the legions from Gaul marched up under Vitellius to dethrone him, and he killed himself to prevent other bloodshed.

When the Eastern army heard of these changes, they declared they would make an Emperor like the soldiers of the West, and hailed Vespasian as Emperor. He left his son Titus to subdue Judea, and set out himself for Italy, where Vitellius had given himself up to riot and feasting. There was a terrible fight and fire in the streets of Rome itself, and the Gauls, who chiefly made up Vitellius' army, did even more mischief than the Gauls of old under Brennus; but at last Vespasian triumphed. Vitellius was taken, and, after being goaded along with the point of a lance, was put to death. There had been eighteen months of confusion, and Vespasian began his reign in the year 70.

It was just then that his son Titus, having taken all the strongholds in Galilee, though they were desperately defended by the Jews, had advanced to besiege Jerusalem. All the Christians had heeded the warning that our blessed Lord had left them, and were safe at a city in the hills called Pella; but the Jews who were left within were fiercely quarrelling among themselves, and fought with one another as savagely as they fought with the enemy. Titus threw trenches round and blockaded the city; and the famine within grew to be most horrible. Some died in their houses, but the fierce lawless zealots rushed up and down the streets, breaking into the houses where they thought food was to be found. When they smelt roasting in one grand dwelling belonging to a lady, they rushed in and asked for the meat, but even they turned away in horror when she uncovered the remains of her own little child, whom she had been eating. At last the Roman engines broke down the walls of the lower city, and with desperate struggling the Romans entered, and found every house full of dead women and children. Still they had the Temple to take, and the Jews had gathered there, fancying that, at the worst, the Messiah would appear and save them. Alas! they had rejected Him long ago, and this was the time of judgment. The Romans fought their way in, up the marble steps, slippery with blood and choked with dead bodies; and fire raged round them. Titus would have saved the Holy Place as a wonder of the world, but a soldier threw a torch through a golden latticed window, and the flame spread rapidly. Titus had just time to look round on all the rich gilding and marbles before it sank into ruins. He took a terrible vengeance on the Jews. Great numbers were crucified, and the rest were either taken to the amphitheatres all over the empire to fight with wild beasts, or were sold as slaves, in such numbers that, cheap as they were, no one would buy them. And yet this wonderful nation has lived on in its dispersion ever since. The city was utterly overthrown and sown with salt, and such treasures as could be saved from the fire were carried in the triumph of Titus — namely, the shew-bread table, the seven-branched candlestick, and the silver trumpets — and laid up as usual among the spoils dedicated to Jupiter. Their figures are to be seen sculptured on the triumphal arch built in honor of Titus, which still stands at Rome.

These Flavian Cæsars were great builders. Much had to be restored at Rome after the two great fires, and they built a new Capitol and new Forum, besides pulling down Nero's Golden House, and setting up on part of the site the magnificent baths known as the Baths of Titus.

ARCH OF TITUS.

Going to the bath, to be steamed, rubbed, anointed, and perfumed by the slaves, was the great amusement of an idle Roman's day, for in the waiting-rooms he met all his friends and heard the news; and these rooms were splendid halls, inlaid with marble, and adorned with the statues and pictures Nero had brought from Greece. On part of the gardens was begun what was then called the Flavian Amphitheatre, but is now known as the Colosseum, from the colossal statue that stood at its door — a wonderful place, with a succession of galleries on stone vaults round the area, on which every rank and station, from the Emperor and Vestal Virgins down to the slaves, had their places, whence to see gladiators and beasts struggle and perish, on sands mixed with scarlet grains to hide the stain, and perfumed showers to overcome the scent of blood, and under silken embroidered awnings to keep off the sun.

Vespasian was an upright man, and though he was stern and unrelenting, his reign was a great relief after the capricious tyranny of the last Claudii. He and his eldest son Titus were plain and simple in their habits, and tried to put down the horrid riot and excess that were ruining the Romans, and they were feared and loved. They had great successes too. Britain was subdued and settled as far as the northern hills, and a great rising in Eastern Gaul subdued. Vespasian was accused of being avaricious, but Nero had left the treasury in such a state that he could hardly have governed without being careful. He died in the year 79, at seventy years old. When he found himself almost gone, he desired to be lifted to his feet, saying that an Emperor should die standing.

VESUVIUS PREVIOUS TO THE ERUPTION OF A.D. 63.

He left two sons, Titus and Domitian. Titus was more of a scholar than his father, and was gentle and kindly in manner, so that he was much beloved. He used to say, "I have lost a day," when one went by without his finding some kind act to do. He was called the delight of mankind, and his reign would have been happy but for another great fire in Rome, which burnt what Nero's fire had left. In his time, too, Mount Vesuvius suddenly woke from its rest, and by a dreadful eruption destroyed the two cities at its foot, Herculaneum and Pompeii. The philosopher Plinius, who wrote on geography and natural history, was stifled by the sulphurous air while fleeing from the showers of stones and ashes cast up by the mountain. His nephew, called Pliny the younger, has left a full account of the disaster, and the cloud like a pine tree that hung over the mountain, the noises, the earthquake, and the fall at last of the ashes and lava. Drusilla, the wife of Felix, the governor before whom St. Paul pleaded, also perished. Herculaneum was covered with solid lava, so that very little could be recovered from it; but Pompeii, being overwhelmed with dust or ashes, was only choked, and in modern days has been discovered, showing perfectly what an old Roman town was like — amphitheatre, shops, bake-houses, and all. Some skeletons have been found: a man with his keys in a cellar full of treasure, a priest crushed by a statue of Isis, a family crowded into a vault, a sentry at his post; and in other cases the ashes perfectly moulded the impression of the figure they stifled, and on pouring plaster into them the forms of the victims have been recovered, especially two women, elder and younger, just as they fell at the gate, the girl with her head hidden in her mother's robe.

PERSECUTION OF THE CHRISTIANS.

Titus died the next year, and his son-in-law Tacitus, who wrote the history of those reigns, laid the blame on his brother Domitian, who was as cruel and savage a tyrant as Nero. He does seem to have been shocked at the wickedness of the Romans. Even the Vestal Virgins had grown shameless, and there was hardly a girl of the patrician families in Rome well brought up enough to become one. The blame was laid on forsaking the old religion, and what the Romans called "Judaising," which meant Christianity, was persecuted again. Flavius Clemens, a cousin of the Emperor, was thus accused and put to death; and probably it was this which led to St. John, the last of the Apostles, being brought to Rome and placed in a cauldron of boiling oil by the Lateran Gate; but a miracle was wrought in his behalf, and the oil did him no hurt, upon which he was banished to the Isle of Patmos.

The Colosseum was opened in Domitian's time, and the shows of gladiators, fights with beasts, and even sea-fights, when the arena was flooded, exceeded all that had gone before. There were fights between women and women, dwarfs and cranes. There is an inscription at Rome which has made some believe that the architect of the Colosseum was one Gandentius, who afterwards perished there as a Christian.

Domitian affronted the Romans by wearing a gold crown with little figures of the gods on it. He did strange things. Once he called together all his council in the middle of the night on urgent business, and while they expected to hear of some foreign enemy on the borders, a monstrous turbot was brought in, and they were consulted whether it was to be cut in pieces or have a dish made on purpose for it. Another time he invited a number of guests, and they found themselves in a black marble hall, with funeral couches, each man's name graven on a column like a tomb, a feast laid as at a funeral, and black boys to wait on them! This time it was only a joke; but Domitian did put so many people to death that he grew frightened lest vengeance should fall on him, and he had his halls lined with polished marble, that he might see as in a glass if any one approached him from behind. But this did not save him. His wife found that he meant to put her to death, and contrived that a party of servants should murder him, A.D. 96.

COIN OF NERO.

CHAPTER XXXIV.
THE AGE OF THE ANTONINES.
96 — 194.

Domitian is called the last of the twelve Cæsars, though all who came after him called themselves Cæsar. He had no son, and a highly esteemed old senator named Cocceius Nerva became Emperor. He was an upright man, who tried to restore the old Roman spirit; and as he thought Christianity was only a superstition which spoiled the ancient temper, he enacted that all should die who would not offer incense to the gods, and among these died St. Ignatius, Bishop of Antioch, who had been bred up among the Apostles. He was taken to Rome, saw his friend St. Polycarp, Bishop of Smyrna, on the way, and wrote him one of a set of letters which remain to this day. He was then thrown to the lions in the Colosseum.

It seems strange that the good Emperors were often worse persecutors than the bad ones, but the fact was that the bad ones let the people do as they pleased, as long as they did not offend them; while the good ones were trying to bring back what they read of in Livy's history, of plain living and high thinking, and shut their ears to knowing more of the Christians than that they were people who did not worship the gods. Moreover, Julius Trajanus, whom Nerva adopted, and who began to reign after him in 98, did not persecute actively, but there were laws in force against the Christians. When Pliny the younger was proprætor of the province of Pontica in Asia Minor, he wrote to ask the Emperor what to do about the Christians, telling him what he had been able to find out about them from two slave girls who had been tortured; namely, that they were wont to meet together at night or early morning, to sing together, and eat what he called a harmless social meal. Trajan answered that he need not try to hunt them out, but that, if they were brought before him, the law must take its course. In Rome, the chief refuge of the Christians was in the Catacombs, or quarries of tufa, from which the city was chiefly built, and which were hollowed out in long galleries. Slaves and convicts worked them, and they were thus made known to the Christians, who buried their dead in places hollowed at the sides, used the galleries for their churches, and often hid there when there was search made for them.

TEMPLE OF ANTONINUS AND FAUSTINA.

Trajan was so good a ruler that he bears the title of Optimus, the Best, as no one else has ever done. He was a great captain too, and conquered Dacia, the country between the rivers Danube, Theiss, and Pruth, and the Carpathian Hills; and he also defeated the Parthians, and said if he had been a younger man he would have gone as far as Alexander. As it was, the empire was at its very largest in his reign, and he was a very great builder and improver, so that one of his successors called him a wall-flower, because his name was everywhere to be seen on walls and bridges and roads — some of which still remain, as does his tall column at Rome, with a spiral line of his conquests engraven round it from top to bottom. He was on his way back from the East when, in 117, he died at Cilicia, leaving the empire to another brave warrior, Publius Ætius Hadrianus, who took the command with great vigor, but found he could not keep Dacia, and broke down the bridge over the Danube. He came to Britain, where the Roman settlements were tormented by the Picts. There he built the famous Roman wall from sea to sea to keep them out. He was wonderfully active, and hastened from one end of the empire to the other wherever his presence was needed. There was a revolt of the Jews in the far East, under a man who pretended to be the Messiah, and called himself the Son of a Star. This was put down most severely, and no Jew was allowed to come near Jerusalem, over which a new city was built, and called after the Emperor's second name, Ælia Capitolina; and, to drive the Jews further away, a temple to Jupiter was built where the Temple had been, and one to Venus on Mount Calvary.

But Hadrian did not persecute, and listened kindly to an explanation of the faith which was shown him at Athens by Quadratus, a Christian philosopher. Hadrian built himself a grand towerlike monument, surrounded by stages of columns and arches, which was to be called the Mole of Hadrian, and still stands, though stripped of its ornaments. Before his death, in 138, he had chosen his successor, Titus Aurelius Antoninus, a good upright man, a philosopher, and 52 years old; for it had been found that youths who became Emperors had their heads turned by such unbounded power, while elder men cared for the work and duty. Antoninus was so earnest for his people's welfare that they called him Pius. He avoided wars, only defended the empire; but he was a great builder, for he raised another rampart in Britain, much further north, and set up another column at Rome, and in Gaul built a great amphitheatre at Nismes, and raised the wonderful aqueduct which is still standing, and is called the Pont du Gard.

His son-in-law, whom he adopted and who succeeded him, is commonly called Marcus Aurelius, as a choice among his many names. He was a deep student and Stoic philosopher, with an earnest longing for truth and virtue, though he knew not how to seek them where alone they could be found; and when earthquake, pestilence and war fell on his empire, and the people thought the gods were offended, he let them persecute the Christians, whose faith he despised, because the hope of Resurrection and of Heaven seemed weak and foolish to him beside his stern, proud, hopeless Stoicism. So the aged Polycarp, Bishop of Smyrna, the last pupil of the Apostles themselves, was sentenced to be burnt in the theatre of his own city, though, as the fire curled round him in a curtain of flame without touching him, he was actually slain with the sword. And in Gaul, especially at Vienne, there was a fearful persecution which fell on women of all ranks, and where Blandina the slave, under the most unspeakable torments, was specially noted for her brave patience.

Aurelius was fighting hard with the German tribes on the Danube, who gave him no rest, and threatened to break into the empire. While pursuing them, he and his army were shut into a strong place where they could get no water, and were perishing with thirst, when a whole legion, all Christian soldiers, knelt down and prayed. A cloud came up, a welcome shower of rain descended, and was the saving of the thirsty host. It was said that the name of the Thundering Legion was given to this division in consequence, though on the column reared by Aurelius it is Jupiter who is shown sending rain on the thirsty host, who are catching it in their shields. After this there was less persecution, but every sort of trouble — plague, earthquake, famine, and war — beset the empire on all sides, and the Emperor toiled in vain against these troubles, writing, meantime, meditations that show how sad and sick at heart he was, and how little comfort philosophy gave him, while his eyes were blind to the truth. He died of a fever in his camp, while still in the prime of life, in the year 180, and with him ended the period of good Emperors, which the Romans call the age of the Antonines. Aurelius was indeed succeeded by his son Commodus, but he was a foolish good-for-nothing youth, who would not bear the fatigues and toils of real war, though he had no shame in showing off in the arena, and is said to have fought there seven hundred and fifty times, besides killing wild beasts. He boasted of having slain one hundred lions with one hundred arrows, and a whole row of ostriches with half-moon shaped arrows which cut off their heads, the poor things being fastened where he could not miss them, and the Romans applauding as if for some noble deed. They let him reign sixteen years before he was murdered, and then a good old soldier named Pertinax began to reign; but the Prætorian Guard had in those sixteen years grown disorderly, and the moment they felt the pressure of a firm hand they attacked the palace, killed the Emperor, cut off his head, and ran with it to the senate-house, asking who would be Emperor. An old senator was foolish enough to offer them a large sum if they would choose him, and this put it into their heads to rush out to the ramparts and proclaim that they would sell the empire to the highest bidder.

A vain, old, rich senator, named Didius Julianus, was at supper with his family when he heard that the Prætorians were selling the empire by auction, and out he ran, and actually bought it at the rate of about £200 to each man. The Emperor being really the commander-in-chief, with other offices attached to the dignity, the soldiers had a sort of right to the choice; but the other armies at a distance, who were really fighting and guarding the empire, had no notion of letting the matter be settled by the Prætorians, mere guardsmen, who stayed at home and tried to rule the rest; so each army chose its own general and marched on Rome, and it was the general on the Danube, Septimius Severus, who got there first; whereupon the Prætorians killed their foolish Emperor and joined him.

MARCUS AURELIUS.

CHAPTER XXXV.
THE PRÆTORIAN INFLUENCE.
197 — 284.

Septimus Severus was an able Emperor, and reigned a long time. He was stern and harsh, as was needed by the wickedness of the time; and he was very active, seldom at Rome, but flashing as it were from one end of the empire to the other, wherever he was needed, and keeping excellent order. There was no regular persecution of the Christians in his time; but at Lyons, where the townspeople were in great numbers Christians, the country-folk by some sudden impulse broke in and made a horrible massacre of them, in which the bishop, St. Irenæus, was killed. So few country people were at this time converts, that Paganus, a peasant, came to be used as a term for a heathen.

Severus was, like Trajan and Hadrian, a great builder and road-maker. The whole empire was connected by a network of paved roads made by the soldiery, cutting through hills, bridging valleys, straight, smooth, and so solid that they remain to this day. This made communication so rapid that government was possible to an active man like him. He gave the Parthians a check; and, when an old man, came to Britain and marched far north, but he saw it was impossible to guard Antonius' wall between the Forth and Clyde, and only strengthened the rampart of Hadrian from the Tweed to the Solway. He died at York, in 211, on his return, and his last watchword was "Labor!" His wife was named Julia Domna, and he left two sons, usually called Caracalla and Geta, who divided the empire; but Geta was soon stabbed by his brother's own hand, and then Caracalla showed himself even worse than Commodus, till he in his turn was murdered in 217.

SEPTIMUS SEVERUS.

ANTIOCH.

His mother, Julia Domna, had a sister called Julia Sæmias, who lived at Antioch, and had two daughters, Sæmias and Mammæa, who each had a son, Elagabalus — so called after the idol supposed to represent the sun, whose priest at Emesa he was — and Alexander Severus. The Prætorian Guard, in their difficulty whom to chose Emperor, chose Elagabalus, a lad of nineteen, who showed himself a poor, miserable, foolish wretch, who did the most absurd things. His feasts were a proverb for excess, and even his lions were fed on parrots and pheasants. Sometimes he would get together a festival party of all fat men, or all thin, all tall, or short, all bald, or gouty; and at others he would keep the wedding of his namesake god and Pallas, making matches between the gods and goddesses all over Italy; and he carried on his service to his god with the same barbaric dances in a strange costume as at Emesa, to the great disgust of the Romans. His grandmother persuaded him to adopt his cousin Alexander, a youth of much more promise, who took the name of Severus. The soldiers were charmed with him; Elagabalus became jealous, and was going to strip him of his honors; but this angered the Prætorians, so that they put the elder Emperor to death in 222.

ALEXANDER SEVERUS.

Alexander Severus was a good and just prince, whose mother is believed to have been a Christian, and he had certainly learned enough of the Divine Law to love virtue, and be firm while he was forbearing. He loved virtue, but he did not accept the faith, and would only look upon our Blessed Lord as a sort of great philosopher, placing His statue with that of Abraham, Orpheus, and all whom he thought great teachers of mankind, in a private temple of his own, as if they were all on a level. He never came any nearer to the faith, and after thirteen years of good and firm government he was killed in a mutiny of the Prætorians in 235.

These guards had all the power, and set up and put down Emperors so rapidly that there are hardly any names worth remembering. In the unsettled state of the empire no one had time to persecute the Christians, and their numbers grew and prospered; in many places they had churches, with worship going on openly, and their Bishops were known and respected. The Emperor Philip, called the Arabian, who was actually a Christian, though he would not own it openly, when he was at Antioch, joined in the service at Easter, and presented himself to receive the Holy Communion; but Bishop Babylas refused him, until he should have done open penance for the crimes by which he had come to the purple, and renounced all remains of heathenism. He turned away rebuked, but put off his repentance; and the next year celebrated the games called the Seculæ, because they took place every Seculum or hundredth year, with all their heathen ceremonies, and with tenfold splendor, in honor of this being Rome's thousandth birthday.

Soon after, another general named Decius was chosen by the army on the German frontier, and Philip was killed in battle with him. Decius wanted to be an old-fashioned Roman; he believed in the gods, and thought the troubles of the empire came of forsaking them; and as the Parthians molested the East, and the Goths and Germans the North, and the soldiers seemed more ready to kill their Emperors than the enemy, he thought to win back prosperity by causing all to return to the old worship, and begun the worst persecution the Church had yet known. Rome, Antioch, Carthage, Alexandria, and all the chief cities were searched for Christians. If they would not throw a handful of incense on the idol's altar or disown Christ, they were given over to all the horrid torments cruel ingenuity could invent, in the hope of subduing their constancy. Some fell, but the greater number were firm, and witnessed a glorious confession before, in 251, Decius and his son were both slain in battle in Mæsia.

TEMPLE OF THE SUN AT PALMYRA.

The next Emperor whose name is worth remembering was Valerian, who had to make war against the Persians. The old stock of Persian kings, professing to be descended from Cyrus, and, like him, adoring fire, had overcome the Parthians, and were spreading the Persian power in the East, under their king Sapor, who conquered Mesopotamia, and on the banks of the Euphrates defeated Valerian in a terrible battle at Edessa. Valerian was made prisoner, and kept as a wretched slave, who was forced to crouch down that Sapor might climb up by his back when mounting on horseback; and when he died, his skin was dyed purple, stuffed, and hung up in a temple.

THE CATACOMBS AT ROME.

The best resistance made to Sapor was by Odenatus, a Syrian chief, and his beautiful Arabian wife Zenobia, who held out the city of Palmyra, on an oasis in the desert between Palestine and Assyria, till Sapor retreated. Finding that no notice was taken of them by Rome, they called themselves Emperor and Empress. The city was very beautifully adorned with splendid buildings in the later Greek style; and Zenobia, who reigned with her young sons after her husband's death, was well read in Greek classics and philosophy, and was a pupil of the philosopher Longinus. Aurelian, becoming Emperor of Rome, came against this strange little kingdom, and was bravely resisted by Zenobia; but he defeated her, made her prisoner, and caused her to march in his triumph to Rome. She afterwards lived with her children in Italy.

Aurelian saw perils closing in on all sides of the empire, and thought it time to fortify the city of Rome itself, which had long spread beyond the old walls of Servius Tullus. He traced a new circuit, and built the wall, the lines of which are the same that still enclose Rome, though the wall itself has been several times thrown down and rebuilt. He also built the city in Gaul which still bears his name, slightly altered into Orleans. He was one of those stern, brave Emperors, who vainly tried to bring back old Roman manners, and fancied it was Christianity that corrupted them; and he was just preparing for a great persecution when he was murdered in his tent, and there were three or four more Emperors set up and then killed almost as soon as their reign was well begun. The last thirty of them are sometimes called the Thirty Tyrants. This power of the Prætorian Guard, of setting up and pulling down their Emperor as being primarily their general, lasted altogether fully a hundred years.

COIN OF SEVERUS

CHAPTER XXXVI.
THE DIVISION OF THE EMPIRE.
284-312.

A Dalmatian soldier named Diocles had been told by a witch that he should become Emperor by the slaughter of a boar. He became a great hunter, but no wild boar that he killed seemed to bring him nearer to the purple, till, when the army was fighting on the Tigris, the Emperor Numerianus died, and an officer named Aper offered himself as his successor. Aper is the Latin for a boar, and Diocles, perceiving the scope of the prophecy, thrust his sword into his rival's breast, and was hailed Emperor by the legions. He lengthened his name out to Diocletianus, to sound more imperial, and began a dominion unlike that of any who had gone before. They had only been, as it were, overgrown generals, chosen by the Prætorians or some part of the army, and at the same time taking the tribuneship and other offices for life. Diocletian, though called Emperor, reigned like the kings of the East. He broke the strength of the Prætorians, so that they could never again kill one Emperor and elect another as before; and he never would visit Rome lest he should be obliged to acknowledge the authority of the Senate, whose power he contrived so entirely to take away, that thenceforward Senator became only a complimentary title, of which people in the subdued countries were very proud.

He divided the empire into two parts, feeling that it was beyond the management of any one man, and chose an able soldier of low birth but much courage, named Maximian, to rule the West from Trier as his capital, while he himself ruled the East from Nicomedia. Each of the two Emperors chose a future successor, who was to rule in part of his dominions under the title of Cæsar, and to reign after him.

DIOCLETIAN.

Diocletian chose his son-in-law Galerius, and sent him to fight on the Danube; and Maximian chose, as Cæsar, Constantius Chlorus, who commanded in Britain, Gaul, and Spain; and thus everything was done to secure that a strong hand should be ready everywhere to keep the legions from setting up Emperors at their own will.

Diocletian was esteemed the most just and kind of the Emperors; Maximian, the fiercest and most savage. He had a bitter hatred of the Christian name, which was shared by Galerius; but, on the other hand, the wife of Diocletian was believed to be a Christian, and Helena, the wife of Constantius, was certainly one. However, Maximian and Galerius were determined to put down the faith. Maximian is said to have had a whole legion of Christians in his army, called the Theban, from the Egyptian Thebes. These he commanded to sacrifice, and on their refusal had them decimated — that is, every tenth man was slain. They were called on again to sacrifice, but still were staunch, and after a last summons were, every man of them, slain as they stood with their tribune Maurice, whose name is still held in high honor in the Engadine. Diocletian was slow to become a persecutor, until a fire broke out in his palace at Nicomedia, which did much mischief in the city, but spared the chief Christian church. The enemies of the Christians accused them of having caused it, and Diocletian required every one in his household to clear themselves by offering sacrifice to Jupiter. His wife and daughter yielded, but most of his officers and slaves held out, and died in cruel torments. One slave was scourged till the flesh parted from his bones, and then the wounds were rubbed with salt and vinegar; others were racked till their bones were out of joint, and others hung up by their hands to hooks, with weights fastened to their feet. A city in Phrygia was surrounded by soldiers and every person in it slaughtered; and the Christians were hunted down like wild beasts from one end of the empire to the other, everywhere save in Britain, where, under Constantius, only one martyrdom is reported to have taken place, namely, that of the soldier at Verulam, St. Alban. It was the worst of all the persecutions, and lasted the longest.

The two Emperors were good soldiers, and kept the enemies back, so that Diocletian celebrated a triumph at Nicomedia; but he had an illness just after, and, as he was fifty-nine years old, he decided that it would be better to resign the empire while he was still in his full strength, and he persuaded Maximian to do the same, in 305, making Constantius and Galerius Emperors in their stead.

DIOCLETIAN IN RETIREMENT.

Constantius stopped the persecution in the West, but it raged as much as ever in the East under Galerius and the Cæsar he had appointed, whose name was Daza, but who called himself Maximin. Constantius fought bravely, both in Britain and Gaul, with the enemies who tried to break into the empire. The Franks, one of the Teuton nations, were constantly breaking in on the eastern frontier of Gaul, and the Caledonians on the northern border of the settlement of Britain. He opposed them gallantly, and was much loved, but he died at York, 305, and Galerius passed over his son Constantine, and appointed a favorite of his own named Licinius. Constantine was so much beloved by the army and people of Gaul that they proclaimed him Emperor, and he held the province of Britain and Gaul securely against all enemies.

Old Maximian, who had only retired on the command of Diocletian, now came out from his retreat, and called on his colleague to do the same; but Diocletian was far too happy on his little farm at Salona to leave it, and answered the messenger who urged him again to take upon him the purple with — "Come and look at the cabbages I have planted." However, Maximian was accepted as the true Emperor by the Senate, and made his son Maxentius, Cæsar, while he allied himself with Constantine, to whom he gave his daughter Fausta in marriage. Maxentius turned out a rebel, and drove the old man away to Marseilles, where Constantine gave him a home on condition of his not interfering with government; but he could not rest, and raised the troops in the south against his son-in-law. Constantine's army marched eagerly against him and made him prisoner, but even then he was pardoned; yet he still plotted, and tried to persuade his daughter Fausta to murder her husband. Upon this Constantine was obliged to have him put to death.

CONSTANTINE THE GREAT.

Galerius died soon after of a horrible disease, during which he was filled with remorse for his cruelties to the Christians, sent to entreat their prayers, and stopped the persecution. On his death, Licinius seized part of his dominions, and there were four men calling themselves Emperors — Licinius in Asia, Daza Maximin in Egypt, Maxentius at Rome, and Constantine in Gaul.

There was sure soon to be a terrible struggle. It began between Maxentius and Constantine. This last marched out of Gaul and entered Italy. He had hitherto seemed doubtful between Christianity and paganism, but a wonder was seen in the heavens before his whole army, namely, a bright cross of light in the noontide sky with the words plainly to be traced round it, *In hoc signo vinces* — "In this sign thou shalt conquer." This sight decided his mind; he proclaimed himself a Christian, and from Milan issued forth an edict promising the Christians his favor and protection. Great victories were gained by him at Turin, Verona, and on the banks of the Tiber, where, at the battle of the Milvian Bridge in 312, Maxentius was defeated, and was drowned in crossing the river. Constantine entered Rome, and was owned by the Senate as Emperor of the West.

CHAPTER XXXVII.
CONSTANTINE THE GREAT.
312-337.

Constantine entered Rome as a Christian, and from his time forward Christianity prevailed. He reigned only over the West at first, but Licinius overthrew Daza, treating him and his family with great barbarity, and then Constantine, becoming alarmed at his power, marched against him, beat him in Thrace, and ten years later made another attack on him. In the battle of Adrianople, Licinius was defeated, and soon after made prisoner and put to death. Thus, in 323, Constantine became the only Emperor.

He was a Christian in faith, though not as yet baptized. He did not destroy heathen temples nor forbid heathen rites, but he did everything to favor the Christians and make Christian laws. Churches were rebuilt and ornamented; Sunday was kept as the day of the Lord, and on it no business might be transacted except the setting free of a slave; soldiers might go to church, and all that had made it difficult and dangerous to confess the faith was taken away. Constantine longed to see his whole empire Christian; but at Rome, heathen ceremonies were so bound up with every action of the state or of a man's life that it was very hard for the Emperor to avoid them, and he therefore spent as little time as he could there, but was generally at the newer cities of Arles and Trier; and at last he decided on founding a fresh capital, to be a Christian city from the first.

The place he chose was the shore of the Bosphorus, where Asia and Europe are only divided by that narrow channel, and where the old Greek city of Byzantium already stood. From hence he hoped to be able to rule the East and the West. He enlarged the city with splendid buildings, made a palace there for himself, and called it after his own name — Constantinople, or New Rome, neither of which names has it ever lost. He carried many of the ornaments of Old Rome thither, but consecrated them as far as possible, and he surrounded himself with Bishops and clergy. His mother Helena made a pilgrimage to Jerusalem, to visit the spots where our blessed Lord lived and died, and to clear them from profanation. The churches she built over the Holy Sepulchre and the Cave of the nativity at Bethlehem have been kept up even to this day.

CONSTANTINOPLE.

There was now no danger in being a Christian, and thus worldly and even wicked men and women owned themselves as belonging to the Church. So much evil prevailed that many good men fled from the sight of it, thinking to do more good by praying in lonely places free from temptation than by living in the midst of it. These were called hermits, and the first and most noted of them was St. Anthony. The Thebaid, or hilly country above Thebes in Egypt, was full of these hermits. When they banded together in brotherhoods they were called monks, and the women who did the like were called nuns.

At this time there arose in Egypt a priest named Arius, who fell away from the true faith respecting our blessed Lord, and taught that he was not from the beginning, and was not equal with God the Father. The Patriarch of Alexandria tried to silence him, but he led away an immense number of followers, who did not like to stretch their souls to confess that Jesus Christ is God. At last Constantine resolved to call together a council of the Bishops and the wisest priests of the whole Church, to declare what was the truth that had been always held from the beginning. The place he appointed for the meeting was Nicea, in Asia Minor, and he paid for the journeys of all the Bishops, three hundred and eighteen in number, who came from all parts of the empire, east and west, so as to form the first Oecumenical or General Council of the Church. Many of them still bore the marks of the persecutions they had borne in Diocletian's time: some had been blinded, or had their ears cut off; some had marks worn on their arms by chains, or were bowed by hard labor in the mines. The Emperor, in purple and gold, took a seat in the council as the prince, but only as a layman and not yet baptized; and the person who used the most powerful arguments was a young deacon of Alexandria named Athanasius. Almost every Bishop declared that the doctrine of Arius was contrary to what the Church had held from the first, and the confession of faith was drawn up which we call the Nicene Creed. Three hundred Bishops at once set their seals to it, and of those who at first refused all but two were won over, and these were banished. It was then that the faith of the Church began to be called Catholic or universal, and orthodox or straight teaching; while those who attacked it were called heretics, and their doctrine heresy, from a Greek word meaning to choose.

The troubles were not at an end with the Council and Creed of Nicea. Arius had pretended to submit, but he went on with his false teaching, and the courtly Bishop Eusebius of Nicomedia, who had the ear of the Emperor, protected him. Athanasius had been made Patriarch, or Father-Bishop, of Alexandria, and with all his might argued against the false doctrine, and cut off those who followed it from the Church.

COUNCIL OF NICEA.

But Eusebius so talked that Constantine fancied quiet was better than truth, and sent orders to Athanasius that no one was to be shut out. This the Patriarch could not obey, and the Emperor therefore banished him to Gaul. Arius then went to Constantinople to ask the Emperor to insist on his being received back to communion. He declared that he believed that which he held in his hand, showing the Creed of Nicea, but keeping hidden under it a statement of his own heresy.

"Go," said Constantine; "if your faith agree with your oath, you are blameless; if not, God be your judge;" and he commanded that Arius should be received to communion the next day, which was Sunday. But on his way to church, among a great number of his friends, Arius was struck with sudden illness, and died in a few minutes. The Emperor, as well as the Catholics, took this as a clear token of the hand of God, and Constantine was cured of any leaning to the Arians, though he still believed the men who called Athanasius factious and troublesome, and therefore would not recall him from exile.

The great grief of Constantine's life was, that he put his eldest son Crispus to death on a wicked accusation of his stepmother Fausta.

CATACOMBS.

On learning the truth, he caused a silver statue to be raised, bearing the inscription, "My son, whom I unjustly condemned;" and when other crimes of Fausta came to light, he caused her to be suffocated.

Baptism was often in those days put off to the end of life, that there might be no more sin after it, and Constantine was not baptized till his last illness had begun, when he was sixty-four years old, and he sent for Sylvester, Pope or Bishop of Rome, where he then was, and received from him baptism, absolution, and Holy Communion. After this, Constantine never put on purple robes again, but wore white till the day of his death in 337.

CHAPTER XXXVIII.
CONSTANTIUS.
337-364.

Constantine the Great left three sons, who shared the empire between them; but two were slain early in life, and only Constantius, the second and worst of the brothers, remained Emperor. He was an Arian, and under him Athanasius, who had returned to Alexandria, was banished again, and took refuge with the Pope Liberius at Rome. Pope — papa in Latin — is the name for father, just as patriarch is; and the Pope had become more important since the removal of the court from Rome; but Constantius tried to overcome Liberius, banished him to Thrace, and placed an Arian named Felix in his room. The whole people of Rome rose in indignation, and Constantius tried to appease them by declaring that Liberius and Felix should rule the Church together; but the Romans would not submit to such a decree. "Shall we have the circus factions in the Church?" they said. "No! one God, one Christ, one Bishop!" In the end Felix was forced to fly, and Liberius kept his seat. Athanasius found his safest refuge in the deserts among the hermits of the Thebaid in Egypt.

Meantime Sapor, king of Persia, was attacking Nisibis, the most Eastern city of the Roman empire, where a brave Catholic named James was Bishop, and encouraged the people to a most brave resistance, so that they held out for four months; and Sapor, thinking the city was under some divine protection, and finding that his army sickened in the hot marshes around it, gave up the siege at last.

Constantius was a little, mean-looking man, but he dressed himself up to do his part as Emperor. He had swarms of attendants like any Eastern prince, most of them slaves, who waited on him as if he was perfectly helpless.

JULIAN.

He had his face painted, and was covered with gold embroidery and jewels on all state occasions, and he used to stand like a statue to be looked at, never winking an eyelid, nor moving his hand, nor doing anything to remind people that he was a man like themselves. He was timid and jealous, and above all others, he dreaded his young cousin Julian, the only relation he had. Julian had studied at Athens, and what he there heard and fancied of the old Greek philosophy seemed to him far grander than the Christianity that showed itself in the lives of Constantius and his courtiers. He was full of spirit and ability, and Constantius thought it best to keep him at a distance by sending him to fight the Germans on the borders of Gaul. There he was so successful, and was such a favorite with the soldiers, that Constantius sent to recall him. This only made the army proclaim him Emperor, and he set out with them across the Danubian country towards Constantinople, but on the way met the tidings that Constantius was dead.

This was in 361, and without going to Rome Julian hastened on to Constantinople, where he was received as Emperor. He no longer pretended to be a Christian, but had all the old heathen temples opened again, and the sacrifices performed as in old times, though it was not easy to find any one who recollected how they were carried on. He said that all forms of religion should be free to every one, but he himself tried to live like an ancient philosopher, getting rid of all the pomp of jewels, robes, courtiers, and slaves who had attended Constantius, wearing simply the old purple garb of a Roman general, sleeping on a lion's skin, and living on the plainest food. Meantime, he tried to put down the Christian faith by laughing at it, and trying to get people to despise it as something low and mean. When this did not succeed, he forbade Christians to be schoolmasters or teachers; and as they declared that the ruin of the Temple of Jerusalem proved our Lord to have been a true Prophet, he commanded that it should be rebuilt. As soon as the foundations were dug, there was an outburst of fiery smoke and balls of flame which forced the workmen to leave off. Such things sometimes happen when long-buried ruins are opened, from the gases that have formed there; but it was no doubt the work of God's providence, and the Christians held it as a miracle.

Julian hated the Catholic Christians worse than the Arians, because he found them more staunch against him. Athanasius had come back to Alexandria, but the Arians got up an accusation against him that he had been guilty of a murder, and brought forward a hand in a box to prove the crime; and though Athanasius showed the man said to have been murdered alive, and with both his hands in their places, he was still hunted out of Alexandria, and had to hide among the hermits of the Thebaid again. When any search was threatened of the spot where he was, the horn was sounded which called the hermits together to church, and he was taken to another hiding-place. Sometimes he visited his flock at Alexandria in secret, and once, when he was returning down the Nile, he learned that a boat-load of soldiers was pursuing him. Turning back, his boat met them. They called out to know if Athanasius had been seen. "He was going down the Nile a little while ago," the Bishop answered. His enemies hurried on, and he was safe.

Julian was angered by finding it impossible to waken paganism. At one grand temple in Asia, whither hundreds of oxen used to be brought to sacrifice, all his encouragement only caused one goose to be offered, which the priest of the temple received as a grand gift. Julian expected, too, that pagans would worship their old gods and yet live the virtuous lives of Christians; and he was disappointed and grieved to find that no works of goodness or mercy sprang from those who followed his belief. He was a kind man by nature, but he began to grow bitter with disappointment, and to threaten when he found it was of no use to persuade; and the Christians expected that there would be a great persecution when he should return from an expedition into the East against the king of Persia.

ARCH OF CONSTANTINE.

He went with a fine army in ships down the Euphrates, and thence marched into Persia, where King Sapor was wise enough to avoid a battle, and only retreat before him. The Romans were half starved, and obliged to turn back. Then Sapor attacked their rear, and cut off their stragglers. Julian shared all the sufferings of his troops, and was always wherever there was danger. At last a javelin pierced him under the arm. It is said that he caught some of his blood in his other hand, cast it up towards heaven, and cried, "Galilean, Thou hast conquered." He died in a few hours, in 363, and the Romans could only choose the best leader they knew to get them out of the sad plight they were in — almost that of the ten thousand Greeks, except that they knew the roads and had friendly lands much nearer. Their choice fell on a plain, honest Christian soldier named Jovian, who did his best by making a treaty with Sapor, giving up all claim to any lands beyond the Tigris, and surrendering the brave city of Nisibis which had held out so gallantly — a great grief to the Eastern Christians. The first thing Jovian did was to have Athanasius recalled, but his reign did not last a year, and he died on the way to Constantinople.

CHAPTER XXXIX.
VALENTINIAN AND HIS FAMILY.
364-392.

When Jovian died, the army chose another soldier named Valentinian, a stout, brave, rough man, with little education, rude and passionate, but a Catholic Christian. As soon as he reached Constantinople, he divided the empire with his brother Valens, whom he left to rule the East, while he himself went to govern the West, chiefly from Milan, for the Emperors were not fond of living at Rome, partly because the remains of the Senate interfered with their full grandeur, and partly because there were old customs that were inconvenient to a Christian Emperor. He was in general just and honest in his dealings, but when he was angry he could be cruel, and it is said he had two bears to whom criminals were thrown. His brother Valens was a weaker and less able man, and was an Arian, who banished Athanasius once more for the fifth time; but the Church of Alexandria prevailed, and he was allowed to remain and die in peace. The Creed that bears his name is not thought to be of his writing, but to convey what he taught. There was great talk at this time all over the cities about the questions between the Catholics and Arians, and good men were shocked by hearing the holiest mysteries of the faith gossiped about by the idlers in baths and market-places.

At this time Damasus, the Pope, desired a very learned deacon of his church, named Jerome, to make a good translation of the whole of the Scriptures into Latin, comparing the best versions, and giving an account of the books. For this purpose Jerome went to the Holy Land, and lived in a cell at Bethlehem, happy to be out of the way of the quarrels at Rome and Constantinople. There, too, was made the first translation of the Gospels into one of the Teutonic languages, namely, the Gothic.

ALEXANDRIA.

The Goths were a great people, of the same Teutonic race as the Germans, Franks, and Saxons — tall, fair, brave, strong, and handsome — and were at this time living on the north bank of the Danube. Many of their young men hired themselves to fight as soldiers in the Roman army; and they were learning Christianity, but only as Arians. It was for them that their Bishop Ulfilas translated the Gospels into Gothic, and invented an alphabet to write them in. A copy of this translation is still to be seen at Upsal in Sweden, written on purple vellum in silver letters.

Another great and holy man of this time was Ambrose, the Archbishop of Milan, who was the guide and teacher of Gratian, Valentinian's eldest son, a good and promising youth so far as he went, but who, after the habit of the time, was waiting to be baptized till he should be further on in life.

GOTHS.

Valentinian's second wife was named Justina; and when he died, as it is said, from breaking a blood-vessel in a fit of rage, in 375, the Western Empire was shared between her little son Valentinian and Gratian.

Justina was an Arian, and wanted to have a church in Milan where she could worship without ascribing full honor and glory to God the Son; but Ambrose felt that the churches were his Master's, not his own to be given away, and filled the Church with Christians, who watched there chanting Psalms day and night, while the soldiers Justina sent to turn them out joined them, and sang and prayed with them.

Gratian did not choose to be called Pontifex Maximus, or chief priest of all the Roman idols, as all the Emperors had been; and this offended many persons. A general named Maximus rose and reigned as Emperor in Britain, and Gratian had too much on his hands in the north to put him down.

In the meantime, a terrible wild tribe called Huns were coming from the West and driving the Goths before them, so that they asked leave from Valens to come across the Danube and settle themselves in Thrace. The reply was so ill managed by Valens' counsellors that the Goths were offended, and came over the river as foes when they might have come as friends; and Valens was killed in battle with them at Adrianople in 378.

Gratian felt that he alone could not cope with the dangers that beset the empire, and his brother was still a child, so he gave the Eastern Empire to a brave and noble Spanish general named Theodosius, who was a Catholic Christian and baptized, and who made peace with the Goths, gave them settlements, and took their young men into his armies. In the meantime, Maximus was growing more powerful in Britain, and Gratian, who chiefly lived in Gaul, was disliked by the soldiers especially for making friends with the young Gothic chief Alaric, whom he joined in hunting in the forests of Gaul in a way they thought unworthy of an Emperor. Finding that he was thus disliked, Maximus crossed the Channel to attack him. His soldiers would not march against the British legions, and he was taken and put to death, bitterly lamenting that he had so long deferred his baptism till now it was denied to him.

Young Valentinian went on reigning at Milan, and Maximus in Gaul. This last had become a Christian and a Catholic in name, but without laying aside his fierceness and cruelty, so that, when some heretics were brought before him, he had them put to death, entirely against the advice of the great Saint and Bishop then working in Gaul, Martin of Tours, and likewise of St. Ambrose, who had been sent by Valentinian to make peace with the Gallic tyrant.

It was a time of great men in the Church. In Africa a very great man had risen up, St. Augustine, who, after doubting long and living a life of sin, was drawn to the truth by the prayers of his good mother Monica, and, when studying in Italy, listened to St. Ambrose, and became a hearty believer and maintainer of all that was good. He became Bishop of Hippo in Africa.

CONVENT ON THE HILLS.

But with the good there was much of evil. All the old cities, and especially Rome, were full of a strange mixture of Christian show and heathen vice. There was such idleness and luxury in the towns that hardly any Romans had hardihood enough to go out to fight their own battles, but hired Goths, Germans, Gauls, and Moors; and these learned their ways of warfare, and used them in their turn against the Romans themselves. Nothing was so much run after as the games in the amphitheatres. People rushed there to watch the chariot races, and went perfectly wild with eagerness about the drivers whose colors they wore; and even the gladiator games were not done away with by Christianity, although these sports were continually preached against by the clergy, and no really devout person would go to the theatres.

Much time was idled away at the baths, which were the place for talk and gossip, and where there was a soft steamy air which was enough to take away all manhood and resolution. The ladies' dresses were exceedingly expensive and absurd, and the whole way of living quite as sumptuous and helpless as in the times of heathenism. Good people tried to live apart. More than ever became monks and hermits; and a number of ladies, who had been much struck with St. Jerome's teaching, made up a sort of society at Rome which busied itself in good works and devotion. Two of the ladies, a mother and daughter, followed him to the Holy Land, and dwelt in a convent at Bethlehem.

Maximus after a time advanced into Italy, and Valentinian fled to ask the help of Theodosius, who came with an army, defeated and slew Maximus, and restored Valentinian, but only for a short time, for the poor youth was soon murdered by a Frank chief in his own service named Arbogastes.

CHAPTER XL.
THEODOSIUS THE GREAT.
392-395.

The Frank, Arbogastes, who had killed Valentinian did not make himself Emperor, but set up a heathen philosopher called Eugenius, who for a little while restored all the heathen pomp and splendor, and opened the temples again, threatening even to take away the churches and turn the chief one at Milan into a stable. They knew that Theodosius would soon come to attack them, so they prepared for a great resistance in the passes of the Julian Alps, and the image of the Thundering Jupiter was placed to guard them.

JULIAN ALPS

Theodosius had collected his troops and marched under the Labarum — that is to say, the Cross of Constantine, which had been the ensign of the imperial army ever since the battle of the Milvian Bridge. It was the cross combined with the two first Greek letters of the name Christ, [Symbol: Greek chi & rho combined], and was carried, as the eagles had been, above a purple silk banner. The men of Eugenius bore before them a figure of Hercules, and in the first battle they gained the advantage, for the more ignorant Eastern soldiers, though Christians, could not get rid of the notion that there was some sort of power in a heathen god, and thought Jupiter and Hercules were too strong for them.

But Theodosius rallied them and led them back, so that they gained a great victory, and a terrible storm and whirlwind which fell at the same time upon the host of Eugenius made the Christian army feel the more sure that God fought on their side. Eugenius was taken and put to death, and Arbogastes fell on his own sword.

Theodosius thus united the empires of the East and West once more. He was a brave and gallant soldier, and a good and conscientious man, and was much loved and honored; but he could be stern and passionate, and he was likewise greatly feared. At Antioch, the people had been much offended at a tax which Theodosius had laid on them; they rose in rebellion, overthrew his statues and those of his family, and dragged them about in the mud. No sooner was this done than they began to be shocked and terrified, especially because of the insult to the statue of the Empress, who was lately dead after a most kind and charitable life. The citizens in haste sent off messengers, with the Bishop at their head, to declare their grief and sorrow, and entreat the Emperor's pardon. All the time they were gone the city gave itself up to prayer and fasting, listening to sermons from the priest, John — called from his eloquence Chrysostom, or Golden Mouth — who preached repentance for all the most frequent sins, such as love of pleasure, irreverence at church, etc. The Bishop on his way met the Emperor's deputies who were charged to enquire into the crime and punish the people; and he redoubled his speed in reaching Constantinople, where he so pleaded the cause of the people that Theodosius freely forgave them, and sent him home to keep a happy Easter with them. This was while he was still Emperor only of the East.

ROMAN HALL OF JUSTICE.

But when he was in Italy with Valentinian, three years later, there was another great sedition at Thessalonica. The people there were as mad as were most of the citizens of the larger towns upon the sports of the amphitheatre, and were vehemently fond of the charioteers whom they admired on either side. Just before some races that were expected, one of the favorite drivers committed a crime for which he was imprisoned. The people, wild with fury, rose and called for his release; and when this was denied to them, they fell on the magistrates with stones, and killed the chief of them, Botheric, the commander of the forces. The news was taken to Milan, where the Emperor then was, and his wrath was so great and terrible that he commanded that the whole city should suffer. The soldiers, who were glad both to revenge their captain and to gain plunder, hastened to put his command into execution; the unhappy people were collected in the circus, and slaughtered so rapidly and suddenly, that when Theodosius began to recover from his passion, and sent to stay the hands of the slayers, they found the city burning and the streets full of corpses.

St. Ambrose felt it his duty to speak forth in the name of the Church against such fury and cruelty; and when Theodosius presented himself at the church door to come to the Holy Communion, Ambrose met him there, and turned him back as a blood-stained sinner unfit to partake of the heavenly feast, and bidding him not add sacrilege to murder.

Theodosius pleaded that David had sinned even more deeply, and yet had been forgiven. "If you have sinned like him, repent like him," said Ambrose; and the Emperor went back weeping to his palace, there to remain as a penitent. Easter was the usual time for receiving penitents back to the Church, but at Christmas the Emperor presented himself again, hoping to win the Bishop's consent to his return at once; but Ambrose was firm, and again met him at the gate, rebuking him for trying to break the rules of the Church.

"No," said Theodosius; "I am not come to break the laws, but to entreat you to imitate the mercy of God whom we serve, who opens the gates of mercy to contrite sinners."

On seeing how deep was his repentance, Ambrose allowed him to enter the Church, though it was not for some time that he was admitted to the Holy Communion, and all that time he fasted and never put on his imperial robes. He also made a law that no sentence of death should be carried out till thirty days after it was given, so as to give time to see whether it were hasty or just.

During this reign another heresy sprang up, denying the Godhead of God the Holy Ghost, and, in consequence, Theodosius called together another Council of the Church, at which was added to the Nicene Creed those latter sentences which follow the words, "I believe in the Holy Ghost." In this reign, too, began to be sung the *Te Deum*, which is generally known as the hymn of St. Ambrose. It was first used at Milan, but whether he wrote it or not is uncertain, though there is a story that he had it sung for the first time at the baptism of St. Augustine.

Theodosius only lived six months after his defeat of Eugenius, dying at Milan in 395, when only fifty years old. He was the last who really deserved the name of a Roman Emperor, though the title was kept up, and Rome had still much to undergo. He left two young sons named Arcadius and Honorius, between whom the empire was divided.

CHAPTER XLI.
ALARIC THE GOTH.
395-410.

The sons of the great Theodosius were, like almost all the children of the Roman Emperors, vain and weak, spoiled by growing up as princes. Arcadius, who was eighteen, had the East, and was under the charge of a Roman officer called Rufinus; Honorius who was only eleven, reigned at Rome under the care of Stilicho, who was by birth a Vandal, that is to say, of one of those Teutonic nations who were living all round the northern bounds of the empire, and whose sons came to serve in the Roman armies and learn Roman habits. Stilicho was brave and faithful, and almost belonged to the imperial family, for his wife Serena was niece to Theodosius, and his daughter Maria was betrothed to the young Honorius.

Stilicho was a very active, spirited man, who found troops to check the enemies of Rome on all sides of the Western Empire. Rufinus was not so faithful, and did great harm in the East by quarrelling with Arcadius' other ministers, and then, as all believed, inviting the Goths to come out of their settlements on the Danube and invade Greece, under Alaric, the same Gothic chief who had been a friend and companion of Gratian, and had fought under Theodosius.

They passed the Danube, overran Macedon, and spread all over Greece, where, being Arian Christians, they destroyed with all their might all the remaining statues and temples of the old pagans; although, as they did not attack Athens, the pagans, who were numerous there, fancied that they were prevented by a vision of Apollo and Pallas Athene. Arcadius sent to his brother for aid, and Stilicho marched through Thrace; Rufinus was murdered through his contrivance, and then, marching on into the Peloponnesus, he defeated Alaric in battle, and drove him out from thence, but no further than Epirus, where the Goths took up their station to wait for another opportunity; but by this time Arcadius had grown afraid of Stilicho, sent him back to Italy with many gifts and promises, and engaged Alaric to be the guardian of his empire, not only against the wild tribes, but against his brother and his minister.

COLONNADES OF SAINT PETER AT ROME.

This was a fine chance for Alaric, who had all the temper of a great conqueror, and to the wild bravery of a Goth had added the knowledge and skill of a Roman general. He led his forces through the Alps into Italy, and showed himself before the gates of Milan. The poor weak boy Honorius was carried off for safety to Ravenna, while Stilicho gathered all the troops from Gaul, and left Britain unguarded by Roman soldiers, to protect the heart of the empire. With these he attacked Alaric, and gained a great victory at Pollentia; the Goths retreated; he followed and beat them again at Verona, driving them out of Italy.

It was the last Roman victory, and it was celebrated by the last Roman triumph. There had been three hundred triumphs of Roman generals, but it was Honorius who entered Rome in the car of victory and was taken to the Capitol, and afterwards there were games in the amphitheatre as usual, and fights of gladiators.

In the midst of the horrid battle a voice was heard bidding it to cease in the name of Christ, and between the swords there was seen standing a monk in his dark brown dress, holding up his hand and keeping back the blows. There was a shout of rage, and he was cut down and killed in a moment; but then in horror the games were stopped. It was found that he was an Egyptian monk named Telemachus, freshly come to Rome. No one knew any more about him, but this noble death of his put an end to shows of gladiators. Chariot races and games went on, though the good and thoughtful disapproved of the wild excitement they caused; but the horrid sports of death and blood were ended for ever.

Alaric was driven back for a time, but there were swarms of Germans who were breaking in where the line of boundary had been left undefended by the soldiers being called away to fight the Goths. A fierce heathen chief named Radegaisus advanced with at least 200,000 men as far as Florence, but was there beaten by the brave Stilicho, and was put to death, while the other prisoners were sold into slavery. But Stilicho, brave as he was, was neither loved nor trusted by the Emperor or the people. Some abused him for not bringing back the old gods under whom, they said, Rome had prospered; others said that he was no honest Christian, and all believed that he meant to make his son Emperor. When he married this son to a daughter of Arcadius, people made sure that this was his purpose. Honorius listened to the accusation, and his favorite Olympius persuaded the army to give up Stilicho. He fled to a church, but was persuaded to come out of it, and was then put to death.

And at that very time Alaric was crossing the Alps. There was no one to make any resistance. Honorius was at Ravenna, safe behind walls and marshes, and cared for nothing but his favorite poultry. Alaric encamped outside the walls of Rome, but he did not attempt to break in, waiting till the Romans should be starved out. When they had come to terrible distress, they offered to ransom their city. He asked a monstrous sum, which they refused, telling him what hosts there were of them, and that he might yet find them dangerous. "The thicker the hay, the easier to mow," said the Goth. "What will you leave us then?" they asked. "Your lives," was the answer.

The ransom the wretched Romans agreed to pay was 5000 pounds' weight of gold and 30,000 of silver, 4000 silk robes, 3000 pieces of scarlet cloth, and 3000 pounds of pepper. They stripped the roof of the temple in the Capitol, and melted down the images of the old gods to raise the sum, and Alaric drew off his men; but he came again the next year, blocked up Ostia, and starved them faster. This time he brought a man named Attalus, whom he ordered them to admit as Emperor, and they did so; but as the governor of Africa would send no corn while this man reigned, the people rose and drove him out, and thus for the third time brought Alaric down on them. The gates were opened to him at night, and he entered Rome on the 24th of August, 410, exactly eight hundred years after the sack of Rome by Brennus.

Alaric did not wish to ruin and destroy the grand old city, nor to massacre the inhabitants; but his Goths were thirsty for the spoil he had kept them from so long, and he gave them leave to plunder for six days, but not to kill, nor to do any harm to the churches. A set of wild, furious men could not, of course, be kept in by these orders, and terrible misfortunes befell many unhappy families; but the mischief done was much less than could have been expected, and the great churches of St. Peter and St. Paul were unhurt. One old lady named Marcella, a friend of St. Jerome, was beaten to make her show where her treasures were; but when at last her tormentors came to believe that she had spent her all on charity, they led her to the shelter of the church with her friends, soon to die of what she had undergone. After twelve days, however, Alaric drew off his forces, leaving Rome to shift for itself. Bishop Innocent was at Ravenna, where he had gone to ask help from the Emperor; but Honorius knew and cared so little that when he was told Rome was lost, he only thought of his favorite hen whose name was Rome, and said, "That cannot be, for I have just fed her."

ALARIC'S BURIAL.

Alaric marched southward, the Goths plundering the villas of the Roman nobles on their way. At Cosenza, in the extreme south, he fell ill of a fever and died. His warriors turned the stream of the river Bionzo out of its course, caused his grave to be dug in the bed of the torrent, and when his corpse had been laid there, they slew all the slaves who had done the work, so that none might be able to tell where lay the great Goth.

CHAPTER XLII.
THE VANDALS.
403.

One good thing came of the Gothic conquest — the pagans were put to silence for ever. The temples had been razed, the idols broken, and no one set them up again; but the whole people of Rome were Christian, at least in name, from that time forth; and the temples and halls of justice began to be turned into churches.

Honorius still lived his idle life at Ravenna, and the Bishop — or, as the Romans called him, Papa, father, or Pope — came back and helped them to put matters into order again. Alaric had left no son, but his wife's brother Ataulf became leader of the Goths. At Rome he had made prisoner Theodosius' daughter Placidia, and he married her; but he did not choose to rule at Rome, because, as he said, his Goths would never bear a quiet life in a city. So he promised to protect the empire for Honorius, and led his tribe away from Italy to Spain, which they conquered, and began a kingdom there. They were therefore known as the Visigoths, or Western Goths.

Arcadius, in the meantime, reigned quietly at Constantinople, where St. John Chrysostom, the golden-mouthed preacher of Antioch, was made Patriarch, or father-bishop. The games and races in the circus at Constantinople were as madly run after as they had ever been at Rome or Thessalonica; there were not indeed shows of gladiators, but people set themselves with foolish vehemence to back up one driver against another, wearing their colors and calling themselves by their names, and the two factions of the Greens and the Blues were ready to tear each other to pieces. The Empress Eudoxia, Arcadius' wife, was one of the most vehement of all, and was, besides, a vain, silly woman, who encouraged all kinds of pomp and expense. St. Chrysostom preached against all the mischiefs that thus arose, so that she was offended, and contrived to raise up an accusation against him and have him driven out of the city. The people of Constantinople still showed so much love for him that she insisted on his being sent further off to the bleak shores of the Black Sea, and on the journey he died, his last words being, "Glory be to God in all things."

ROMAN CLOCK.

Arcadius died in 408, leaving a young son, called Theodosius II., in the care of his elder sister Pulcheria, under whom the Eastern Empire lay at peace, while the miseries of the Western went on increasing. New Emperors were set up by the legions in the distant provinces, but were soon overthrown, while Honorius only remained at Ravenna by the support of the kings of the Teuton tribes; and as he never trusted them or kept faith with them, he was always offending them and being punished by fresh attacks on some part of his empire, for which he did not greatly care so long as they let him alone.

Ataulf died in Spain, and Placidia came back to Ravenna, where Honorius gave her in marriage to a Roman general named Constantius, and she had a son named Valentinian, who, when his uncle died after thirty-seven years of a wretched reign, became Emperor in his stead, under his mother's guardianship, in 423.

Two great generals who were really able men were her chief supporters — Boniface, Count or Commander of Africa; and Aëtius, who is sometimes called the last of the Romans, though he was not by birth a Roman at all, but a Scythian. He gained the ear of the Empress Placidia, and persuaded her that Boniface wanted to set himself up in Africa as Emperor, so that she sent to recall him, and evil friends assured him that she meant to put him to death as soon as he arrived. He was very much enraged, and though St. Augustine, now an old man, who had long been Bishop of Hippo, advised him to restrain his anger, he called on Genseric, the chief of the Vandals, to come and help him to defend his province.

The Vandals were another tribe of Teutons — tall, strong, fair-haired, and much like the Goths, and, like them, they were Arians. They had marauded in Italy, and then had followed the Goths to Spain, where they had established themselves in the South, in the country called from them Vandalusia, or Andalusia. Their chief was only too glad to obey the summons of Boniface, but before he came the Roman had found out his mistake; Placidia had apologized to him, and all was right between them. But it was now too late; Genseric and his Vandals were on the way, and there was nothing for it but to fight his best against them.

SPANISH COAST.

He could not save Carthage, and, though he made the bravest defence in his power, he was driven into Hippo, which was so strongly fortified that he was able to hold it out a whole year, during which time St. Augustine died, after a long illness. He had caused the seven penitential Psalms to be written out on the walls of his room, and was constantly musing on them. He died, and was buried in peace before the city was taken. Boniface held out for five years altogether before Africa was entirely taken by the Vandals, and a miserable time began for the Church, for Genseric was an Arian, and set himself to crush out the Catholic Church by taking away her buildings and grievously persecuting her faithful bishops.

Valentinian III, made a treaty with him, and even yielded up to him all right to the old Roman province of Africa; but Genseric had a strong fleet of ships, and went on attacking and plundering Sicily, Corsica, Sardinia, Italy and the coasts of Greece.

Britain, at the same time, was being so tormented by the attacks of the Saxons by sea, and the Caledonians from the north, that her chiefs sent a piteous letter to Aëtius in Gaul, beginning with "The groans of the Britons;" but Aëtius could send no help, and Gaul itself was being overrun by the Goths in the south, the Burgundians in the middle, and the Franks in the north, so that scarcely more than Italy itself remained to Valentinian.

VANDALS PLUNDERING

The Eastern half of the Empire was better off, though it was tormented by the Persians in the East, on the northern border by the Eastern Goths or Ostrogoths, who had stayed on the banks of the Danube instead of coming to Italy, and to the south by the Vandals from Africa. But Pulcheria was so wise and good that, when her young brother Theodosius II. died without children, the people begged her to choose a husband who might be an Emperor for them. She chose a wise old senator named Marcian, and when he died, she again chose another good and wise man named Zeno; and thus the Eastern Empire stood while the West was fast crumbling away. The nobles were almost all vain, weak cowards, who only thought of themselves, and left strangers to fight their battles; and every one was cowed with fear, for a more terrible foe than any was now coming on them.

PYRAMIDS AND SPHINX IN EGYPT.

CHAPTER XLIII.
ATTILA THE HUN
435-457.

The terrible enemy who was coming against the unhappy Roman Empire was the nation of Huns, a wild, savage race, who were of the same stock as the Tartars, and dwelt as they do in the northern parts of Asia, keeping huge herds of horses, spending their life on horseback, and using mares' milk as food. They were an ugly, small, but active race, and used to cut their children's faces that the scars might make them look more terrible to their enemies. Just at this time a great spirit of conquest had come upon them, and they had, as said before, driven the Goths over the Danube fifty years ago, and seized the lands we still call Hungary. A most mighty and warlike chief called Attila had become their head, and wherever he went his track was marked by blood and flame, so that he was called "The Scourge of God." His home was on the banks of the Theiss, in a camp enclosed with trunks of trees, for he did not care to dwell in cities or establish a kingdom, though the wild tribes of Huns from the furthest parts of Asia followed his standard — a sword fastened to a pole, which was said to be also his idol.

He threatened to fall upon the two empires, and an embassy was sent to him at his camp. The Huns would not dismount, and thus the Romans were forced to address them on horseback. The only condition upon which he would abstain from invading the empire was the paying of an enormous tribute, beyond what almost any power of theirs could attempt to raise. However, he did not then attack Italy, but turned upon Gaul. So much was he hated and dreaded by the Teutonic nations, that all Goths, Franks, and Burgundians flocked to join the Roman forces under Aëtius to drive him back. They came just in time to save the city of Orleans from being ravaged by him, and defeated him in the battle of Chalons with a great slaughter; but he made good his retreat from Gaul with an immense number of captives, whom he killed in revenge.

HUNNISH CAMP.

The next year he demanded that Valentinian's sister, Honoria, should be given to him, and when she was refused, he led his host into Italy and destroyed all the beautiful cities of the north. A great many of the inhabitants fled into the islands among the salt marshes and pools at the head of the Adriatic Sea, between the mouths of the rivers Po and Adige, where no enemy could reach them; and there they built houses and made a town, which in time became the great city of Venice, the queen of the Adriatic.

Aëtius was still in Gaul, the wretched Valentinian at Ravenna was helpless and useless, and Attila proceeded towards Rome. It was well for Rome that she had a brave and devoted Pope in Leo. I., who went out at the head of his clergy to meet the barbarian in his tent, and threaten him with the wrath of Heaven if he should let loose his cruel followers upon the city. Attila was struck with his calm greatness, and, remembering that Alaric had died soon after plundering Rome, became afraid. He consented to accept of Honoria's dowry instead of herself, and to be content with a great ransom for the city of Rome. He then turned to his camp on the Danube with all his horde, and soon after his arrival he married a young girl whom he had made prisoner. The next morning he was found dead on his bed in a pool of his own blood, and she was gone; but as there was no wound about him, it was thought that he had broken a blood-vessel in the drunken fit in which he fell asleep, and that she had fled in terror. His warriors tore their cheeks with their daggers, saying that he ought to be mourned only with tears of blood; but as they had no chief as able and daring as he, they gradually fell back again to their north-eastern settlements, and troubled Europe no more.

ST. MARK'S, VENICE.

Valentinian thought the danger over, and when Aëtius came back to Ravenna, he grew jealous of his glory and stabbed him with his own hand. Soon after he offended a senator named Maximus, who killed him in revenge, became Emperor, and married his widow, Eudoxia, the daughter of Theodosius II. of Constantinople, telling her that it was for love of her that her husband was slain. Eudoxia sent a message to invite the dreadful Genseric, king of the Vandals, to come and deliver her from a rebel who had slain the lawful Emperor. Genseric's ships were ready, and sailed into the Tiber; while the Romans, mad with terror, stoned Maximus in their streets. Nobody had any courage or resolution but the Pope Leo, who went forth again to meet the barbarian and plead for his city; but Genseric being an Arian, had not the same awe of him as the wild Huns, hated the Catholics, and was eager for the prey. He would accept no ransom instead of the plunder, but promised that the lives of the Romans should be spared. This was the most dreadful calamity that Rome, once the queen of cities, had undergone. The pillage lasted fourteen days, and the Vandals stripped churches, houses, and all alike, putting their booty on board their ships; but much was lost in a storm between Italy and Africa. The golden candlestick and shew-bread table belonging to the Temple at Jerusalem were carried off to Carthage with the spoil, and no less than sixty thousand captives, among them the Empress Eudoxia, who had been the means of bringing in Genseric, with her two daughters. The Empress was given back to her friends at Constantinople, but one of her daughters was kept by the Vandals, and was married to the son of Genseric. After plundering all the south of Italy, Genseric went back to Africa without trying to keep Rome or set up a kingdom; and when he was gone, the Romans elected as Emperor a senator named Avitus, a Gaul by birth, a peaceful and good man.

THE POPE'S HOUSE.

His daughter had married a most excellent Gaulish gentleman named Sidonius Apollinaris, who wrote such good poetry that the Romans placed his bust crowned with laurel in the Capitol. He wrote many letters, too, which are preserved to this time, and show that, in the midst of all this crumbling power of Rome, people in Southern Gaul managed to have many peaceful days of pleasant country life. But Sidonius' quiet days came to an end when, layman and lawyer as he was, the people of Clermont begged him to be their Bishop. The Church stood, whatever fell, and people trusted more to their Bishop than to any one else, and wanted him to be the ablest man they could find. So Sidonius took the charge of them, and helped them to hold out their mountain city of Clermont for a whole year against the Goths, and gained good terms for them at last, though he himself had to suffer imprisonment and exile from these Arian Goths because of his Catholic faith.

CHAPTER XLIV.
THEODORIC THE OSTROGOTH.
457 — 561.

Avitus was a good man, but the Romans grew weary of him, and in the year 457 they engaged Ricimer, a chief of the Teutonic tribe called Suevi, to drive him out, when he went back to Gaul, where he had a beautiful palace and garden. After ten months Ricimer chose another Sueve to be Emperor. He had been a captain under Aëtius, and had the Roman name of Majorian. He showed himself brave and spirited; led an army into Spain and attacked Genseric; but he was beaten, and came back disappointed. Ricimer was, however, jealous of him, forced him to resign, and soon after poisoned him.

After this, Ricimer really ruled Italy, but he seemed to have a sort of awe of the title of Cæsar Augustus, the Emperor, for he forbore to use it himself, and gave it to one poor weak wretch after another until his death in 472. His nephew went on in the same course; but at last a soldier named Orestes, of Roman birth, gained the chief power, and set up as Emperor his own little son, whose Christian name was Romulus Augustus, making him wear the purple and the crown, and calling him by all the titles; but the Romans made his name into Augustulus, or Little Augustus. At the end of a year, a Teutonic chief named Odoacer crossed the Alps at the head of a great mixture of different German tribes, and Orestes could make no stand against him, but was taken and put to death. His little boy was spared, and was placed at Sorrento; but Odoacer sent the crown and robes of the West to Zeno, the Eastern Emperor, saying that one Emperor was enough. So fell the Roman power in 476, exactly twelve centuries after the date of the founding of Rome. It was thought that this was meant by the twelve vultures seen by Romulus, and that the seven which Remus saw denoted the seven centuries that the Republic stood. It was curious, too, that it should be with the two names of Romulus and Augustus that Rome and her empire fell.

Odoacer called himself king, and, indeed, the Western Empire had been nearly all seized by different kings — the Vandal kings in Africa, the Gothic kings in Spain and Southern Gaul, the Burgundian kings and Frank kings in Northern Gaul, the Saxon kings in Britain. The Ostro or Eastern Goths, who had since the time of Valens dwelt on the banks of the Danube, had been subdued by Attila, but recovered their freedom after his death. One of their young chiefs, named Theodoric, was sent as a hostage to Constantinople, and there learned much. He became king of the Eastern Goths in 470, and showed himself such a dangerous neighbor to the Eastern Empire that, to be rid of him the Emperor Zeno advised him to go and attack Odoacer in Italy. The Ostrogoths marched seven hundred miles, and came over the Alps into the plains of Northern Italy, where Odoacer fought with them bravely, but was beaten. They besieged him even in Ravenna, till after three years he was obliged to surrender and was put to death.

ROMULUS AUGUSTUS RESIGNS THE CROWN.

Rome could make no defence, and fell into Theodoric's hands with the rest of Italy; but he was by far the best of the conquerors — he did not hurt or misuse them, and only wished his Goths to learn of them and become peaceful farmers. He gave them the lands which had lost their owners; about thirty or forty thousand families were settled there by him on the waste lands, and the Romans who were left took courage and worked too. He did not live at Rome, though he came thither and was complimented by the Senate, and he set a sum by every year for repairing the old buildings; but he chiefly lived at Verona, where he reigned over both the Eastern and Western Goths in Gaul and Italy.

He was an Arian, but he did not persecute the Catholics, and to such persons as changed their profession of faith to please him he showed no more favor, saying that those who were not faithful to their God would never be faithful to their earthly master. He reigned thirty-three years, but did not end as well as he began, for he grew irritable and distrustful with age; and the Romans, on the other hand, forgot that they were not the free, prosperous nation of old, and displeased him. Two of their very best men, Boëthius and Symmachus, were by him kept for a long time prisoners at Rome and then put to death. While Boëthius was in prison at Pavia, he wrote a book called *The Consolations of Philosophy*, so beautiful that the English king Alfred translated it into Saxon four centuries later. Theodoric kept up a correspondence with the other Gothic kings wherever a tribe of his people dwelt, even as far as Sweden and Denmark; but as even he could not write, and only had a seal with the letters [Greek: THEOD] with which to make his signature, the whole was conducted in Latin by Roman slaves on either side, who interpreted to their masters. An immense number of letters from Theodoric's secretary are preserved, and show what an able man his master was, and how well he deserved his name of "The Great." He died in 526, leaving only two daughters. Their two sons, Amalric and Athalaric, divided the Eastern and Western Goths between them again.

Seven Gothic kings reigned over Northern Italy after Theodoric. They were fierce and restless, but had nothing like his strength and spirit, and they chiefly lived in the more northern cities — Milan, Verona, and Ravenna, leaving Rome to be a tributary city to them, where there still remained the old names of Senate and Consuls, but the person who was generally most looked up to and trusted was the Pope. All this time Rome was leavening the nations who had conquered her. When they tried to learn civilized ways, it was from her; they learned to speak her tongue, never wrote but in Latin, and worshipped with Latin prayers and services. Far above all, these conquerors learned Christianity from the Romans. When everything else was ruined, the Bishop and clergy remained, and became the chief counsellors and advisers of many of these kings.

It was just at this time that there was living at Monte Casino, in the South of Italy, St. Benedict, an Italian hermit, who was there joined by a number of others who, like him, longed to pray for the sinful world apart rather than fight and struggle with bad men. He formed them into a great band of monks, all wearing a plain dark dress with a hood, and following a strict rule of plain living, hard work, and prayers at seven regular hours in the course of the day and night. His rule was called the Benedictine, and houses of monks arose in many places, and were safe shelters in these fierce times.

CHAPTER XLV.
BELISARIUS.
533-563.

The Teutonic nations soon lost their spirit when they had settled in the luxurious Roman cities, and as they were as fierce as ever, their kings tore one another to pieces. A very able Emperor, named Justinian, had come to the throne in the East, and in his armies there had grown up a Thracian who was one of the greatest and best generals the world has ever seen. His name was Belisarius, and strange to say, both he and the Emperor had married the daughters of two charioteers in the circus races. The Empress was named Theodora, the general's wife Antonina, and their acquaintance first made Belisarius known to Justinian, who, by his means, ended by winning back great part of the Western Empire.

He began with Africa, where Genseric's grandson was reigning over the Vandals, and paying so little heed to his defences that Belisarius landed without any warning, and called all the multitudes of old Roman inhabitants to join him, which they joyfully did. He defeated the Vandals in battle, entered Carthage, and restored the power of the empire. He brought away the golden candlestick and treasures of the Temple, and the cross believed to be the true one, and carried them to Constantinople, whence the Emperor sent them back to the Church of the Holy Sepulchre at Jerusalem.

Just as Belisarius had returned to Constantinople, a piteous entreaty came to Justinian from Amalosontha, the daughter of Theodoric, who had been made prisoner by Theodotus, the husband she had chosen. It seemed to be opening a way for getting back Italy, and Justinian sent off Belisarius; but before he had sailed, the poor Gothic queen had been strangled in her bath. Belisarius, however, with 4500 horse and 3000 foot soldiers, landed in Sicily and soon conquered the whole island, all the people rejoicing in his coming. He then crossed to Rhegium, and laid siege to Naples. As usual, the inhabitants were his friends, and one of them showed him the way to enter the city through an old aqueduct which opened into an old woman's garden.

NAPLES.

Theodotus was a coward as well as a murderer, and fled away, while a brave warrior named Vitiges was proclaimed king by the Goths at Rome. But with the broken walls and all the Roman citizens against him, Vitiges thought it best not to try to hold out against Belisarius, and retreated to Ravenna, while Rome welcomed the Eastern army as deliverers. But Vitiges was collecting an army at Ravenna, and in three months was besieging Rome again. Never had there been greater bravery and patience than Vitiges showed outside the walls of Rome, and Belisarius inside, during the summer of 536. There was a terrible famine within; all kinds of strange food were used in scanty measure, and the Romans were so impatient of suffering, that Belisarius was forced to watch them day and night to prevent them betraying him to the enemy. Indeed, while the siege lasted a whole year, nearly all the people of Rome died of hunger and wretchedness; and the Goths, in the unhealthy Campagna around, died of fevers and agues, until they, too, had all perished except a small band, which Vitiges led back to Ravenna, whither Belisarius followed him, besieged him, made him prisoner, and carried him to Constantinople. Justinian gave him an estate where he could live in peace.

CONSTANTINOPLE.

The Moors in Africa revolted, and Belisarius next went to subdue them. While he was there, the Goths in Italy began to recover from the blow he had given them, and chose a brave young man named Totila to be their king. In a very short time he had won back almost all Italy, for there really were hardly any men left, and even Justinian had only two small armies to dispose of, and those made up of Thracians and Isaurians from the shores of the Black Sea. One of these was sent with Belisarius to attack the Goths, but was not strong enough to do more than just hold Totila in check, and Justinian would not even send him all the help possible, because he dreaded the love the army bore to him. After four years of fighting with Totila he was recalled, and a slave named Narces, who had always lived in the women's apartment in the palace, was sent to take the command. He was really able and skilled, and being better supported, he gained a great victory near Rome, in which Totila was killed, and another near Naples, which quite overcame the Ostrogoths, so that they never became a power again. Italy was restored to the Empire, and was governed by an officer from Constantinople, who lived at Ravenna, and was called the Exarch.

Belisarius, in the meantime, was sent to fight with the king of Persia, Chosroës, a very warlike prince, who had overrun Syria and carried off many prisoners from Antioch. Belisarius gained victory after victory over him, and had just driven him back over the rivers, when again came a recall, and Narses was sent out to finish the war. Theodora, the Empress, wanted to reign after her husband, and had heard that, on a report coming to the army of his death, Belisarius had said that he should give his vote for Justin, the right heir. So she worked on the fears all Emperors had — that their troops might proclaim a successful general as Emperor, and again Belisarius was ordered home, while Narses was sent to finish what he had begun.

There was one more war for this great man when the wild Bulgarians invaded Thrace, and though his soldiers were little better than timid peasants, he drove them back and saved the country. But Justinian grew more and more jealous of him, and, fancying untruly that he was in a plot for placing Justin on the throne, caused him to be thrown into prison, and sent him out from thence stripped of everything, and with his eyes torn out. He found a little child to lead him to a church door, where he used to sit with a wooden dish before him for alms. When it was known who the blind beggar was, there was such an uproar among the people that Justinian was obliged to give him back his palace and some of his riches; but he did not live much longer.

Though Justinian behaved so unjustly and ungratefully to this great man and faithful servant, he is noted for better things, namely, for making the Church of St. Sophia, or the Holy Wisdom, which Constantine had built at Constantinople, the most splendid of all buildings, and for having the whole body of Roman laws thoroughly overlooked and put into order. Many even of the old heathen laws were very good ones, but there were others connected with idolatry that needed to be done away with; and in the course of years so many laws and alterations had been made, that it was the study of a lifetime even to know what they were, or how to act on them. Justinian set his best lawyers to put them all in order, so that it might be more easy to work by them. The Roman citizens in Greece, Italy, and all the lands overrun by the Teutonic nations were still judged by their own laws, so that this was a very useful work; and it was so well done that the conquerors took them up in time, and the Roman law was the great model studied everywhere by those who wished to understand the rules of jurisprudence, that is, of law and justice. Thus in another way Rome conquered her conquerors.

Justinian died in 563, and was succeeded by his nephew Justin, whose wife Sophia behaved almost as ill to Narses as Theodora had done to Belisarius, for while he was doing his best to defend Italy from the savage tribes who were ready at any moment to come over the Alps, she sent him a distaff, and ordered him back to his old slavery in the palace.

CHAPTER XLVI.
POPE GREGORY THE GREAT.
563 — 800.

No sooner was Narses called home than another terrible nation of Teutones, who had hitherto dwelt in the North, began to come over the Alps. These were the Longbeards, or Lombards, as they were more commonly called; fierce and still heathen. Their king, Alboin, had carried off Rosamond, the daughter of Kunimund, king of the Gepids, another Teutonic tribe. There was a most terrible war, in which Kunimund was killed and all his tribe broken up and joined with the Lombards. With the two united, Alboin invaded Italy and conquered all the North. Ravenna, Verona, Milan, and all the large towns held out bravely against them, but were taken at last, except Venice, which still owned the Emperor at Constantinople. Alboin had kept the skull of Kunimund as a trophy, and had had it set in gold for a drinking-cup, as his wild faith made him believe that the reward of the brave in the other world would be to drink mead from the skulls of their fallen enemies. In a drunken fit at Verona, he sent for Rosamond and made her pledge him in this horrible cup. She had always hated him, and this made her revenge her father's death by stabbing him to the heart in the year 573. The Lombard power did not, however, fall with him; his nephew succeeded him, and ruled over the country we still call Lombardy. Rome was not taken by them, but was still in name belonging to the Emperor, though he had little power there, and the Senate governed it in name, with all the old magistrates. The Prætor at the time the Lombards arrived was a man of one of the old noble families, Anicius Gregorius, or, as we have learned to call him, Gregory. He had always been a good and pious man, and while he took great care to fulfil all the duties of his office, his mind was more and more drawn away from the world, till at last he became a monk of St. Benedict, gave all his vast wealth to build and endow monasteries and hospitals, and lived himself in an hospital for beggars, nursing them, studying the Holy Scriptures, and living only on pulse, which his mother sent him every day in a silver dish — the only remnant of his wealth — till one day, having nothing else to give a shipwrecked sailor who asked alms, he bestowed it on him.

POPE GREGORY THE GREAT.

He was made one of the seven deacons who were called Cardinal Deacons, because they had charge of the poor of the principal parishes of Rome; and it was when going about on some errand of kindness that he saw the English slave children in the market, and planned the conversion of their country; but the people would not let him leave Rome, and in 590, the Senate, the clergy, and the people chose him Pope. It was just then that a terrible pestilence fell on Rome, and he made the people form seven great processions — of clergy, of monks, of nuns, of children, of men, of wives, and of widows — all singing litanies to entreat that the plague might be turned away. Then it was that he beheld an angel standing on the tomb of Hadrian, and the plague ceased. Ever after, the great old tomb has been called the Castle of St. Angelo.

THE POPE'S PULPIT.

It was a troublous time, but Gregory was so much respected that he was able to keep Rome orderly and safe, and to make peace between the Emperor Maurice and the Lombards' king, Agilulf, who had an excellent wife, Theodolinda. She was a great friend of the Pope, wrote a letter to him, and did all she could to support him. The Eastern Empire was still owned at Rome, but when there was an attempt to make out that the Patriarch of Constantinople was superior to the Pope, Gregory upheld the principle that no Patriarch had any right to be above the rest, nor to be called Universal Bishop. Gregory was a very great man, and the justice and wisdom of his management did much to make the Romans look to their Pope as the head of affairs even after his death in 604.

BATTLE OF TOURS.

The Greek Empire sent an officer to govern the extreme South of Italy, which, like Rome and Venice, still owned the Emperor; but all the troops that could be hired were soon wanted to fight with the Arabs, whose false prophet Mahommed had taught them to spread religion with the sword. There was no one capable of making head against the Lombards, and the Popes only kept them off by treaties and good management; and at last, in 741, Pope Gregory III. put himself under the protection of Charles Martel, the great Frank captain who had beaten the Mahometans at the battle of Tours. Charles Martel was rewarded by being made a Roman senator, so was his son Pippin, who was also king of the Franks, and his grandson Charles the Great, who had to come often to Italy to protect Rome, and at last broke up the Lombard kingdom, was chosen Roman Emperor as of old, and crowned by Pope Leo III. in the year 800. From that time there was again the Western Empire, commonly called the Holy Roman Empire, the Emperor, or Cæsar — Kaisar, as the Germans still call him — being generally also king of Germany and king of Lombardy. Rome was all this time chiefly under the power of the Popes, who grew in course of years to be more and more of princes, and at the same time to claim more power over the Church, calling themselves Universal Bishops contrary to the teaching of St. Gregory the Great. All this, however, belongs to the history of Europe in modern times, and will be found in the history of Germany, since there were many struggles between the Popes and Emperors. For Rome has really had *two* histories, and those who visit Rome and study the wonderful buildings there may dwell on the old or the new, the pagan or the Christian, as their minds lead them, or else on that strange middle time when idolatry and Christianity were struggling together.

www.ingramcontent.com/pod-product-compliance
Lightning Source LLC
Chambersburg PA
CBHW032128010526
44111CB00033B/221